This PROMISE of CHANGE

This
PROMISE of
CHANGE

ONE GIRL'S STORY
IN THE FIGHT FOR
SCHOOL EQUALITY

JO ANN ALLEN BOYCE
and
DEBBIE LEVY

BLOOMSBURY
CHILDREN'S BOOKS
NEW YORK LONDON OXFORD NEW DELHI SYDNEY

BLOOMSBURY CHILDREN'S BOOKS
Bloomsbury Publishing Inc., part of Bloomsbury Publishing Plc
1385 Broadway, New York, NY 10018

BLOOMSBURY, BLOOMSBURY CHILDREN'S BOOKS, and the Diana logo
are trademarks of Bloomsbury Publishing Plc

First published in the United States of America in January 2019
by Bloomsbury Children's Books

Bloomsbury books may be purchased for business or promotional use. For information
on bulk purchases please contact Macmillan Corporate and Premium Sales Department
at specialmarkets@macmillan.com

Library of Congress Cataloging-in-Publication Data
Names: Boyce, Jo Ann Allen, author. | Levy, Debbie, author.
Title: This promise of change : one girl's story in the fight for school equality /
by Jo Ann Allen Boyce and Debbie Levy.
Description: New York : Bloomsbury Children's Books, 2019.
Identifiers: LCCN 2018026349 (print) | LCCN 2018047038 (e-book)
ISBN 978-1-68119-852-1 (hardcover) • ISBN 978-1-68119-853-8 (e-book)
Subjects: LCSH: Boyce, Jo Ann Allen—Juvenile literature. | African American
teenage girls—Tennessee—Clinton—Biography—Juvenile literature. |
African American students—Tennessee—Clinton—Biography—Juvenile literature. |
School integration—Tennessee—Clinton—Juvenile literature. | Clinton (Tenn.)—
Race relations—Juvenile literature.
Classification: LCC F444.C68 B69 2019 (print) | LCC F444.C68 (e-book) |
DDC 379.2/630976873—dc23
LC record available at https://lccn.loc.gov/2018026349

Interior design by Kay Petronio
Typeset by Westchester Publishing Services
Printed and bound in the U.S.A. by Berryville Graphics Inc., Berryville, Virginia
2 4 6 8 10 9 7 5 3 1

To find out more about our authors and books visit www.bloomsbury.com and
sign up for our newsletters.

To all humankind who've experienced
the pain of injustice and inequality.

In memory of my parents, Herbert and Alice Josephine
Hopper Allen: your courage, wisdom, love, and belief
in me continues to sustain me; and my brother,
Herbert Howard: I miss you; I miss your genius.

For my children, Victor H., London, Kamlyn: my
greatest and most beloved accomplishments, for your
support of and help in writing this book; and my
grandchildren, D'mitri, Cameron, Maya, and Shia: my
beacons of hope, the lights of my life, for loving Nana
so much and inspiring me to always tell my story.

"Education is the most powerful weapon
which you can use to change the world."
—*Nelson Mandela*

—J. A. B.

✦———⚸———✦

With admiration for and gratitude
to the twelve students of Clinton, Tennessee,
who boldly took their rightful places.

—D. L.

CONTENTS

INTRODUCTION

⟫——⟨——⟪

The U.S. Constitution says that all American citizens are guaranteed "equal protection of the laws." For years, though, the laws of many states required black children and white children to go to separate schools. In Southern states especially—where racist traditions had deep roots in centuries of black slavery that endured until the end of the Civil War—many whites could not abide the thought of their children attending school with black children. Lawmakers, who were uniformly white, would not spend public monies to create good schools for black children. So African American students were forced to attend schools with inferior buildings, supplies, books, and facilities.

This type of racial segregation and discrimination in education, required and enforced by state law, was the norm well into the twentieth century. Despite the Constitution's "equal protection" guarantee, the U.S. Supreme Court found no constitutional defect in segregation. To the contrary, in 1896, in the case of *Plessy v. Ferguson*, the Court said that facilities that were racially "separate" could be considered "equal"—or at least equal enough.

Decades later, in 1954, came *Brown v. Board of Education*. In that case, the Supreme Court reversed the position it had held in a line of cases since *Plessy*. Those old decisions were wrong, the justices ruled. "Separate but equal" schools were *not* equal. They were not equal even if the buildings, supplies, books, and facilities of schools for black children were brought up to par with schools for whites. Racially segregated schools deprived African American children of equal educational opportunities and were unconstitutional—period.

And so, what next?

A Supreme Court ruling is a big deal, but it cannot enforce itself. White lawmakers and white citizens were in no hurry to desegregate their schools. Some states passed laws to punish people who attempted to comply with *Brown v. Board*. Some made plans to shut down their public school systems rather than allow black and white children to go to school together.

If *Brown v. Board*'s promise of change was to become reality, people had to take action. In the small town of Clinton, in eastern Tennessee, a group of twelve African American high school students stepped up.

This is the story of one girl among those twelve.

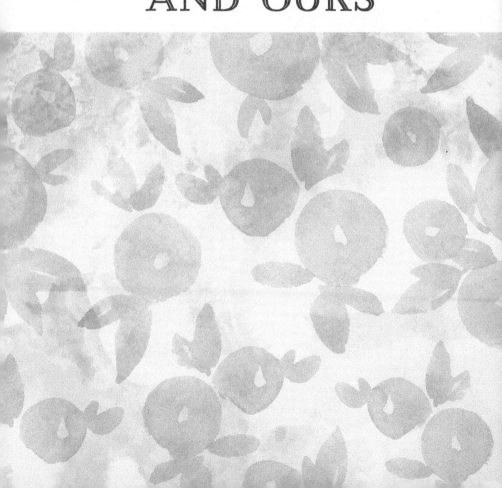

PART 1

MINE, THEIRS, AND OURS

CLINTON, TENNESSEE: MY TOWN
(FALL 1955)

DON'T HURRY THRU TOWN

**GIVE US A CHANCE
TO BE FRIENDLY**

—A sign at the city limits

Up on the Hill—
Foley Hill, some say, but we just say *the Hill*—
we look down
on downtown—

not looking down our noses,
just looking down from our Hill, where we live.

We have the high ground here,
here on the Hill,
once called Freedmen's Hill
after ex-slaves moved here
when they became *ex-*
way back when the Civil War ended.
Those six hundred climbed the Hill north of town
and built their homes.
Now the Hill is my neighborhood.
Clinton is my town.
Anderson County is my county.
Tennessee is my state.

Up on the Hill
we have all sorts of homes,
nice and not-so-nice, mixed up together.
Mine is nice.
At least, I think so.
We have all sorts of neighbors,
nice and not-so-nice, mixed up together.
My family is nice,
and I don't say that just because they're my family.
Mom says Daddy knows no strangers—
which is a clever way of saying that he knows *everyone*.
Mom is quieter, but
you can borrow a cup of sugar anytime from our kitchen
and never have to pay it back.

Up on the Hill
we have Friday night fish fries at our church,
trout crisped up crunchy in great big pots of hot oil on the fire,
kids running around in the churchyard—
because how much fish can a kid stand to eat?—
ball games when there's still light,
hide-and-seek in the cemetery after dark.
And the big treat, the special only-at-the-fish-fry treat:
bottles of red soda pop
with peanuts in the bottom.
I look out for Mamie, my little sister,
and Herbie, our baby brother,
because I'm the fourteen-year-old,
and because I don't mind.

Up on the Hill
we have concerts,
gospel music sung by famous gospel singers,
like Clara Ward herself—
in person!
Clara Ward and the Ward Singers
have been on television and
at Carnegie Hall in New York City and
at our very own church.
"Surely, God Is Able," they sing,
and "How I Got Over,"
wearing gowns glittery with sequins,

hair swept in updos way high on their heads—
that is not something you see in church
every day.

Up on the Hill
we put on plays and musicales;
it's Alice Josephine Allen at the piano (that's my mother),
Herbert Allen (that's my father) singing out in his deep voice,
and Jo Ann (that's me)—and Mamie!—in the youth choir,
my family fitting in nice and tight here

up on the Hill,
where my town is a friendly fine town.

CLINTON, TENNESSEE:
THEIR TOWN

I'm not so much an "us" and "them" girl,
but I didn't make the rules and the rules draw lines
between us
and them.

Their town is friendly and fine too—
with white people friendly and fine
to each other as they go about
the business of running the town,
the schools, the businesses,
and going to theaters and restaurants as they please;

and friendly and fine
to black people who stay in our places.
And we do stay in our places,
which is always
a place where we know
friendly white smiles
can turn upside down

in a quick minute
if we try to move these lines
between white and black,
and don't you forget it.

I know something about their town
because my mother has worked for a white family—
the Crenshaws—
for twenty-five years, ever since she was sixteen.
They treat her nicely
and she treats them nicely.
Mom cooks for their family,
making fancy dishes from Mrs. Crenshaw's recipe book
when they have company,
dishes like chicken divan with asparagus,
which she comes home and makes for us, too.
Delicious!
Almost as delicious as my mother's fried chicken.
Almost as delicious as my father's fluffy biscuits.
Mmm-hmm, they both can cook.

Mom keeps house for the Crenshaws too,
and it's a house with a room full of books,
one entire room filled with books—
You remember I said my house is nice.
Well, it's not nice enough
to have a library

right at home.
I would like that, one day.

I used to sit in the Crenshaws' library and read
when I was a little girl
and my mother brought me with her to her job.
Even today she brings home books
that the Crenshaw family is done with.
My favorite ever is *The Robe*,
a story that shows just how much
Jesus had to put up with,
and just how strong
Jesus had to be
to go through what He went through,
and yet still He said:
Love thy neighbor.

If my house were overflowing with books,
and I needed to make room
for more books, or clothes, or furniture,
I would find a book other than
The Robe to give up,
but if Mrs. Crenshaw had to part with it,
I'm glad it found its way to me.

On the Hill we all know something about their town
because we all have a mother

or aunt or sister or cousin
who works as a maid or a cook
for a white family.
We all have a father, an uncle, a brother
who does yard work or handyman work
for a white family,
and we all see
what it would be like to be more free
in where we go, how we speak, what we can do.

I would like that, one day, too.

CLINTON: OUR TOWN

3,500 white people

+

220 black people

+

1 movie theater, where Negroes may only sit in the balcony

+

1 swimming pool, where Negroes may not go at all

+

1 fun rec center, with bowling alleys, ping-pong tables, badminton—but not for Negroes

+

1 public library (only, Negroes aren't part of the "public")

+

1 public high school (whites only)

+

1 drugstore, where Negroes may buy things but may not linger and definitely may not sit and eat at the lunch counter where, I hear, they serve chicken salad sandwiches made from roosters not hens

+

0 restaurants where Negroes may eat

=

Segregation.

Separate, not equal.

Segregation.

The way it is and always has been.

I try to look at the good side of things, 'cause
there's nothing I can do about the bad,
so . . .

. . . we may not sit where we want at the movies,
swim in the pool, go to the rec center, library, restaurants—
but
we have our own
churches, two of them:
Easter parade, everyone looking fine in new outfits;
gym at the Negro elementary school,
where all us kids hang out;
neighborhood, where everyone looks out for everyone;

and this is the good side of things,
which I wouldn't trade
just for a better seat at the movies.

We don't need white people
to be our friends.

We like the friends we have,
thank you very much!
But we get along with the white family
across the street from us, the Smiths—
yes, the Hill has a few white folks,
called "white trash" by some other white folks in town,
who I suppose can't imagine living this near to us.
When Mrs. Smith runs out of flour or sugar
she knows she can fill up a measuring cup or two
at our house.
When Mr. Smith goes deer hunting
he shares the meat with us.
Mrs. Smith makes the best
home fried potatoes, crusty and salty,
served with sweet tomatoes from her backyard garden,
and we eat them with her kids,
Ruby, George, and Riley,
in her kitchen.
I call this neighborly, not trashy.

Blacks and whites in Clinton mostly get along well enough,
I think.
We are civilized to one another.
It's not like in Biloxi, down in Mississippi,
where we hear that Negroes have to step off the sidewalk
when the white people walk by.
Imagine that.

The worst for me, I'd say,
is the feeling I get at Hoskins Drugstore,
where my friends and I go
after the school bus drops us off
at the end of the long ride back
from where we go to high school
at the Negro high school
clear over in Knoxville.
The feeling is that I better hurry up,
buy my candy bar and get out,
because they want our money
but don't really want us as customers.
I go in because my friends do,
but the candy isn't as sweet as it was
when I was younger
and didn't notice the bitter taste.

WELCOME TO CLINTON
"A WONDERFUL PLACE TO LIVE"
GOOD FISHING ON NORRIS LAKE

—*Another sign at the city limits*

KEEP YOUR HEAD UP

When I taste the bitter,
when I feel the pain
from the daily slights
like a spreading stain . . .

From "No Coloreds" here
to "Whites Only" there,
from the genteel chains
that we're forced to wear—

"You're good as anyone"—
the words my parents say.
"God has made us equal."
Our prayers show me the way.
Grandmother's always told me
"You keep your head up high"—

These words,
those thoughts,
this faith—

They lift me up.
I fly.

MY SCHOOLS

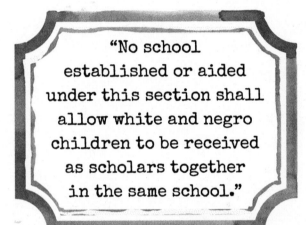

> "No school
> established or aided
> under this section shall
> allow white and negro
> children to be received
> as scholars together
> in the same school."

*—Constitution of Tennessee,
Article XI, Section 12*

I. The Green McAdoo Grammar School

Itty-bitty
not real pretty.
On our Hill, not in the city.

Two rooms hold grades one to eight;
pretty hard to regulate,

so no one blames dear Miss Blair
when she shows up behind a chair
and *whooosh!* gives a swat—not a hit, just a swat—
'cause, *sheesh,* that's the way to shush the boys up!

Don't get the wrong idea:
Miss Blair loves her students so,
but she's got to keep the chitchat down
to teach them what to know.

II. What I Know
about Green McAdoo Grammar School,
where I walked to school
for first, second, third, fourth, fifth,
sixth, seventh, and eighth grades:

First, they once called it the Clinton Colored School.

Second, it's only for Negro students.

Third, it was renamed for Mr. Green L. McAdoo
(yes, his first name was Green)
who was a Buffalo Soldier,
which doesn't mean he fought buffalo,
but that he was a black member of the United States Army.

Fourth, before Green McAdoo,

before Clinton Colored School,
the Freedmen's Bureau built a school
after the Civil War
on the very same site here on the Hill,
also for Negroes only,
and white folks burned it down
out of hate.
But then it was rebuilt
and the rebuilding was led by two men—
one who used to own slaves,
and the other who used to be a slave.

Fifth, isn't history strange?
Strange as folks.

Sixth, Green McAdoo had no cafeteria, no gymnasium,
and no indoor bathrooms
until the time I started first grade.
The grammar school in town did,
and also had separate classrooms for every grade,
but that school was whites-only,
and still is.

Seventh, two little classrooms for eight grades of children,
outdated books cast off from the whites-only school,
old desks carved so deeply with someone else's initials
that your pencil pokes through your paper

into the canyon of that carving—
none of this is good enough.

But eighth: I loved that itty-bitty
not real pretty
school up on the Hill.

III. Last Year: Vine Junior High
Ninth grade:
not in Clinton,
not if you're a black kid.
Negroes want more education?
Leave town.

This school,
far from Clinton,
twisty roads to Knoxville.
Bumps in the ride, lumps in my throat.
Don't cry.

New kids,
not so friendly.
Felt so lost. Felt so dumb.
Small-town girl meets big-city school—
I cried.

Separate.

Segregated.
That's why we were sent here.
If *race* should make me feel at home,
it failed.

IV. This Year: Austin High School
Tenth grade:
not in Clinton,
not if you're a black kid.
Negroes want to go to high school?
Knoxville!

New school,
same bumpy roads,
but no more tears for me.
I'm stronger than I was before:
I'll live.

I live.
I give it time.
I give this place a chance.
Big-city school and small-town girl
make friends.

THEIR SCHOOL

Clinton High School,
a fine-looking building,
with brick and clean white trim.
We walk by it
   every day
      on our way
         to the bus
      that picks us up
   to drive us
twenty miles
   on crooked roads,
      that wash out in a storm,
         around the mountain,
      down the valley
   to Austin High School
for Negroes only
   over in Knoxville
      in a whole other county.

Clinton High School.

Here it is, right here, right close, right down the Hill,
with its solid red brick and clean white trim
for white students only.
We walk by it, not to it,
because it's their school,
big,
but not big enough
for twelve Negro students
who look at it every day
but have never been inside.

"Section 11395. *Unlawful for white and colored persons to attend same school.* It shall be unlawful for any school, academy, college, or other place of learning to allow white and colored persons to attend the same school, academy, college, or other place of learning.

"Section 11396. *Unlawful for teacher to allow such mixed attendance or to teach them in same class.* It shall be unlawful for any teacher, professor, or educator in any college, academy, or school of learning, to allow the white and colored races to attend the same school, or for any teacher or educator, or other person to instruct or teach both the white and colored races in the same class, school, or college building, or in any other place or places of learning, or allow or permit the same to be done with their knowledge, consent, or procurement.

"*Section 11397. Violation is a misdemeanor; fine and imprisonment.* Any person violating any of the provisions of this article, shall be guilty of a misdemeanor, and, upon conviction, shall be fined for each offense fifty dollars, and imprisonment not less than thirty days nor more than six months."

—The Code of Tennessee

OURS:
JANUARY 1956

There is no Mr. Brown V. Board
like there is
Mr. Green L. McAdoo,
but there is *Brown v. Board of Education.*
It's a ruling by the Supreme Court of the United States
and it says

separate schools for black kids and white kids are
unconstitutional.
It says
segregation in education is
so unequal,
so unfair
that it's against the law,
not just any old law,
but the highest law in the whole country—
that is, the United States Constitution.

Brown v. Board is law, higher

than the laws in Clinton
that say there are white schools and black schools.
Brown v. Board makes those rules
against the rules.

Here's the thing:
Brown v. Board isn't news to any of us—
the Supreme Court made this ruling back in 1954.
But the leaders of Clinton have been acting
as though it were the law
for other people in other places—
not for us, not for our town.

So here we are,
in the new year of 1956,
we black high school kids
still riding a bus to a faraway black school,
leaving Clinton High behind
in the rearview mirror,
white as it's always been.

But here's what's new:
Judge Taylor over in Knoxville
has told Clinton's officials
that they can't ignore *Brown v. Board*
anymore.
Clinton High School

must be integrated—
not someday, not eventually,
but in the next fall term.

It will be *ours*,
blacks and whites.
Desegregated, not segregated.
Ours.
Theirs.
Mine.

"No state shall . . . deny to any person within its
jurisdiction the equal protection of the laws."

—*United States Constitution,
Amendment XIV, adopted 1868*

"We conclude that, in the field of public education, the doctrine of 'separate but equal' has
no place. Separate educational facilities are
inherently unequal."

—*U.S. Supreme Court decision of May 17, 1954,
in* Brown v. Board of Education

"It is the opinion of this Court that desegregation as to high school students in that county
should be effected by a definite date and that
a reasonable date should be fixed as one not
later than the beginning of the fall term of
the present year of 1956."

—*Ruling of Judge Robert L. Taylor of January 4, 1956,*
applying the rule of Brown v. Board *to Clinton,*
Tennessee, and Clinton High School

"INTEGRATION OF COUNTY HIGH SCHOOLS IS
ORDERED BY START OF 1956 SCHOOL YEAR"

—*Front page banner headline,*
Clinton Courier-News, *January 5, 1956*

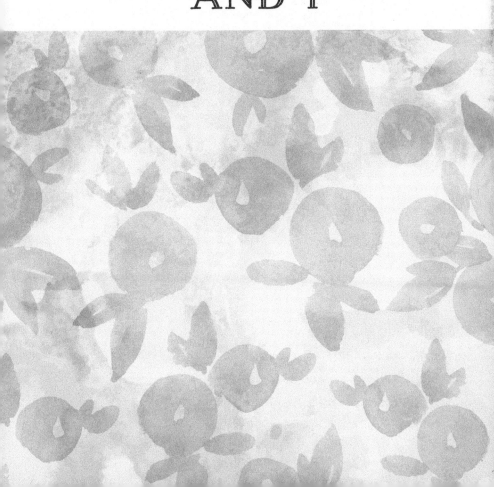

PART 2

ME, MYSELF, AND I

ME, MYSELF, AND I

Billie Holiday sings the song,
"Me, Myself, and I."
I. Myself. Me. You.
See me. Can you try?

Clinton High kids,
who will you see?
A "Negro girl"?
The genuine me?
The me who laughs,
the me who sings,
the me who prays,
the me with wings.
Will you see me?
Outside and in?
Mind. Heart. Soul. Skin.

Me, myself, and I
are very much like you.
Daughter, sister, neighbor, friend—
See me, through and through.

MY MOTHER MAKES
SOME RULES

Ain't
Crazy, man
Cool it
Daddy-O!
Don't have a cow
Don't bug me
Like wow
No sweat
Razz my berries

are words you'll never hear me say,
no matter what school I attend,
segregated or integrated—
nope.
You won't hear me say that, either.
Not "nope."
No.

If we use words that are not proper English,
Mom just about has a cow.
If she knew I said "has a cow,"

she would have a cow.

It's like wow.

"Don't you know how to speak the King's English?" she says,

by which she means

proper grammar and diction,

not a royal accent.

Crazy, man, right?

Yeah.

Only not yeah.

"The word is *yes*," she says.

What really rattles her cage is

ain't.

Mom says she will wash our mouths out with soap if we say

ain't.

So we ain't never gonna say it.

(I'm just trying to razz your berries.)

We shall never say it.

Why does Mom get bugged by all this?

Why doesn't she just cool it on the grammar?

Why isn't she just, No sweat, Daddy-O,

speak however you like?

Doesn't she know

the kids at Green McAdoo

used to tease me and Mamie

because of the way we talk?

"You think you're Mrs. Crenshaw!"
they would taunt.
Meaning,
You think you're white.

Mom told us that she stopped going to school
when she was sixteen.
She needed to pitch in to earn money
to help her family.
She put her sister and brother through college
by working as a maid.
But that doesn't mean she has to sound ignorant
and her children definitely don't have to sound ignorant
and they should get the best education they can get
and it should show.

Yes, ma'am.

MY MOTHER BREAKS
SOME RULES

Not the rules of grammar—
O, Heaven forfend!

But *dig this,*
I mean,
consider this:

The rules of shopping in Clinton are unwritten
but known to all.
Negroes are not banned from stores,
but at the grocery store downtown,
if a white person is in the bread aisle,
we wait.
We do not enter that aisle
while the white person is contemplating
baked goods.
This is not a bread rule, you understand;
it applies to milk and scouring powder, too.

At the Ritz Theatre,

when we go to see a movie (from the balcony,
according to the rules),
we may enter the front door to buy candy and popcorn,
but we must then walk outside with our food
to enter a separate door
that leads to the stairs
to the buzzard's roost.

These are the rules.
We follow them
and they keep us safe.
We don't like them.
We don't like suspecting—
knowing, really—
that white people in Clinton are nice enough to us
so long as we follow the rules,
so long as we are not—
hate to say it, even think it—
"uppity."

The rule in the hat shop—
the millinery shop, as someone speaking
the King's English might say—
is that if a colored woman absolutely must shop for a hat,
then she must put a scarf on her head
before trying it on.
The milliner, and her white customers,

do not want Negro heads,
Negro hair,
touching a hat
that a white woman might later put on her own head.
O, Heaven forfend!

One day, my mother wanted to shop for a new hat,
but she didn't want to put on a scarf
to shield the hat from her Negro head,
so she didn't.

The sky did not fall.
The wrath of white Clinton did not come tumbling down
upon her unscarfed head
because my mother looks rather like a white woman.
My mother, like her mother, could pass—
and although that is not how she lives,
although she would never deny who she is—
that day, when another customer said to Mom,
"Where did you get your beautiful tan?"
Mom answered that the tan came naturally,

which was true enough.

My mother is bold
and strict
and beautiful.

11

BIG SISTER, LITTLE SISTER

I have been known
to use my fists
in defense of Mamie,
which is also in defense of me,
when those kids at Green McAdoo taunted,
"You think you're Mrs. Crenshaw!"
No, she doesn't.
No, we don't.

We have to follow our mother's rule,
which is also Miss Blair's rule—
Miss Blair, who also speaks the King's English.
Mamie loves Miss Blair as much as I do.
I've seen Mamie line her dolls up in our room,
and they become her students,
and she speaks to them very properly.
You'd best believe
those dolls learn how to speak proper English.

The real kids,

the kids who aren't dolls lined up on the floor,
they just don't *get* it,
just as they don't *get* that if we were to say,
"You just don't *git* it!"—
which is how a lot of people talk in Clinton,
no matter where they live and what their color—
our mother would chastise and correct us:
"You can say the letter *e* in *get*,
so say it!"

You think you're white.
Fighting words
when aimed at my little sister
by kids who ought to know that
Ain't none of us thinks we're white.
Pardon me, Mother. Excuse me, Miss Blair.

12

LITTLE SISTER, BIG SISTER

I have been known
to use my hands
on Mamie
when she does the one thing
I don't like about her:
tattling—
on her own sister!

When Mamie saw me holding hands
with Robert Willis,
our minister's son,
my great crush,
who is older than me
and done with high school—
she said she would tell our parents.
I grabbed her, pushed her
up against our screen door,
and warned her that I would hurt her
if she told.
She knew I would,

because once before
I'd taken her hair
and rolled it
through the washing-machine roller
out on the back porch.

I'm not proud of this.
It's not the genuine me.
And I didn't get away with it.
Mamie may have learned the rule
that sisters don't tattle,
but our neighborhood doesn't follow that rule.
It has eyes and ears
and everyone looks after everyone
like I look after Mamie,
and looking after me
meant someone told my parents and . . .
my parents have been known
to use a switch
from the sycamore tree
to teach me a lesson.

And I *get* it.

13

SINGING SISTERS

Mostly Mamie and I
get along famously,
and we sing famously too
(at our church, anyway).
The Allen sisters sing duets
for special church occasions,
like the Easter service
when we performed
"In the Garden."

I come to the garden alone
While the dew is still on the roses;
And the voice I hear,
Falling on my ear;
The Son of God discloses.

And He walks with me, and He talks with me,
And He tells me I am His own,
And the joy we share as we tarry there,
None other has ever known.

I love that—
it's a joy I share
with the best little sister
any big sister could have.

14

ABOUT CHURCH

When I say we go to church,
I don't mean we go to a service
for an hour on Sunday.
I mean
Sunday school
morning service
evening service
maybe a special program
for visiting choirs or preachers or speakers.

You don't miss church
at Reverend Willis's Mt. Sinai Baptist.
You don't say,
Oh, I don't feel like going,
even though sometimes I don't feel like going.
But mostly I like it.
I like the singing.
I like seeing my church friends.
And I like seeing Robert Willis,
Reverend Willis's son.

From church I learned
that all people come
from the same Source.
We are all created by God.
Black, white, yellow, red, brown.
Equal.
So when someone says an ugly word about us
because we are black,
I know they are ignorant.
Ignorant of God,
ignorant of what it means
to be one of God's children;

I know they are backward,
and I look forward.

15

ANOTHER THING ABOUT CHURCH

Church means
prayer.
It means
song.
It also means
time with my best friend, Gail Ann Epps,
who doesn't live on the Hill
(not all black folks do),
but who does belong to Mt. Sinai Baptist,
so church time
is Jo Ann, Gail Ann time.

There's a game we play
on the church steps,
a game of two teams,
two players each—
me and my sister, Mamie,
against
Gail Ann and her sister, Sandra.
One team member sits on the top step,

the other stands on the step below,
    holding out her hands,
        hiding a marble in one fist.
            The sitter has to guess the fist—
                guess correctly, the players move down a step.
Guess wrong, stay where you are.

Mamie and I take turns on the steps;
Gail Ann and Sandra take turns on the steps.
    The stander becomes the sitter.
        Back and forth the turns go,
            and the team to reach the bottom first—
                winner, winner!

I know: simple.
Too simple for us high school students.
Maybe even too simple for our little sisters!
Go ahead and think we're simple.
Sometimes simple
is exactly what we want,
playing like little children
on a Sunday afternoon
at church.
Sometimes simple
is exactly what we need,
when complicated is showing its face
just around the corner.

PART 3

GETTING READY
(MAY TO AUGUST 1956)

EASY
(MAY 1956)

They do seem to be trying
to make it simple for us.

The principal and a teacher
from Clinton High School
come up the Hill,
to our old classroom at Green McAdoo,
for a meeting with us and our parents.
They're nice.
Principal Brittain.
Mrs. Anderson.

We take achievement tests,
the same tests,
they tell us,
that white students take
before starting at Clinton High.

They gather up the tests.

Another day, Mrs. Anderson returns
to Green McAdoo.
She helps us each choose classes
based on how we did on the tests.
We fill out forms.
So now we're preregistered.

Simple as the step game.
Easy-peasy.
Step, step,
    winner, winner.
        We're in!

A COMPLICATION

We're in, yes.
But it's more complicated than that.
Or, looked at another way—it's simpler.

Our lives at Clinton High School will be
small.
We'll go to school.
We'll leave school.

While we're choosing classes with Mrs. Anderson,
our parents are asking Principal Brittain some questions.
May our children play on sports teams against other schools?
No, because those other schools are white.

May our children enjoy social events at school—
mixers, sock hops, parties?
No, because the other students are white.
There will be no "mixed social events."
You may come to our school,
the principal says,

because that is what the law requires,
but you'll stay in your group,
and we'll stay in ours.

We'll go to school.
We'll leave school.
Just like we do now at Austin High,
where none of the other students is white
and we're free
to join sports teams and after-school clubs,
attend pep rallies and football games—
except not really free,
because when that bus leaves Knoxville
to drive twenty miles
back to Clinton
at the end of the school day,
that's that.
It's not coming back until the next morning.

You can't stay after school
when you have no ride home.
Glee club, football, cheerleading?
No, no, and no.

You can't stay after school,
when the fun stuff is whites-only.
Glee club, football, cheerleading?

No, no, and no.

Simple. That's the complication.

.... ✦ ....

"In discussing social activities Mr. Brittain
said he told the parents of the negro students
'we are not going to have mixed social events.
You may come, but you must stay in your
own group and we will stay in ours. . . .
We think the community should know that
we are following the orders of the courts. We
believe that loyal Americans must always do
so. . . .'"

—*"Clinton High Plans For Integration,"*
Clinton Courier-News, *August 9, 1956*

STANDING IN LINE, 1
(MONDAY, AUGUST 20)

These are the names:
Alfred Williams
Alvah Jay McSwain
Anna Theresser Caswell
Bobby Cain
Gail Ann Epps
Maurice Soles
Minnie Ann Dickey
Regina Turner
Robert Thacker
Ronald Gordon Hayden
William Latham

And: Jo Ann Allen.
Me.

These are the names
to be registered at Clinton High School.
We're past the private meetings on the Hill,
past testing, class selection, preregistration,

past disappointing answers.
It's final registration.
It's a first.
We stand in line
at our new school,
we twelve Negro students
among hundreds of white students,
some of whom stare
but say nothing unkind
or kind.
We say nothing also.

I think this is going to work out.
I am an optimist.
Like my dad,
I like to think
people will do the right thing.
Like my dad,
I see the good in people,
and I think they will see the good in me.
I think they will see me,
not just the
"Negro girl."

I like to think so,
but I know
that doesn't make it so.

STANDING IN LINE, 2

This all feels downright momentous.
But is it also momentary?
The newspaper has a big advertisement
by the Tennessee Federation for Constitutional Government:
They don't want the school desegregated,
and they are asking everybody else who doesn't want
quote mixed schools *unquote*
to join them in seeking
quote an orderly solution to this problem *unquote*.

Who *are* these people,
the Tennessee Federation for Constitutional Government?
The Supreme Court interprets the Constitution
for all the United States,
including Tennessee,
and the Supreme Court has said the Constitution requires
quote unquote mixed schools.
So we have
"an orderly solution to this problem" already.
Don't we?

And those white students looking at us lined up
with them
to register,
saying nothing unkind
or kind—
I know that their parents and our white neighbors
and the school board and the newspaper editor
and Principal Brittain
and every
single
white
person I can think of
didn't want to open Clinton High to us.

I know they fought Alvah Jay McSwain's mother
for five years
when she brought a lawsuit
against our separate-but-not-equal Negro schools,
even before *Brown v. Board,*
and they would have kept fighting,
kept insisting on their all-white school
for another five years,
maybe another fifty years,
if the Supreme Court hadn't spoken.

But the Supreme Court did speak.
And so the school board stopped fighting.

The newspaper editor stopped arguing.
The mayor and the police chief and the sheriff
and the principal—
they're all getting ready for us.
Maybe not exactly getting ready to *welcome* us,
but to accept our right to go to *our* school.

So this *is* momentous.
Not merely momentary.
I am an optimist;
I choose to be.

20

STANDING IN LINE, 3

My family and I spend a lot of time in church,
and it's not all Friday night fish fries and musicales.
We read the Bible,
so I know the Book of Exodus begins with the words
These are the names,
and there follow the names of the twelve sons of Israel,
Reuben, Simeon, Levi, and Judah,
Issachar, Zebulun, and Benjamin,
Dan and Naphtali, Gad and Asher,
and Joseph.

And in time, the Bible says, that generation passed away
and their children had children
and those children had children, and on it went until
a new pharaoh rose up in Egypt
who knew not Joseph,
and who put all those descendants of Israel
to work at hard bondage:
slavery.

We Negroes in Clinton, Tennessee,

our ancestors have seen slavery,

lived slavery,

and we're done with that.

Unlike those twelve sons of Israel,

we twelve sons and daughters of Clinton will not have

descendants in slavery.

That's over.

That's not me being optimistic.

That's the gospel truth.

These are our names:

Alfred, Alvah Jay, Anna,

Bobby, Gail Ann, Maurice, Minnie Ann, Regina, Robert,

Poochie (that's what we call Ronald), William (Billy).

And me, Jo Ann.

Now we're registered for our school.

And eight hundred white students,

they're also registered for our school.

I don't know their names,

except for the Smith boys, who live across the street—

Riley and George—

but I hope to get to know their names,

and to know them—

maybe even make friends with them!—

starting one week from today,
when we return to this building
for the first day of school.

"We have never heard anyone in Clinton say he wanted the integration of students in the schools, but we have heard a great many of the people say: 'We believe in the law. We will obey the ruling of the Court. We have no other lawful choice.'"

—Editorial in the Clinton Courier-News
written by editor Horace V. Wells Jr.,
August 30, 1956

21

BEST FRIENDS

One name
among the twelve names
is closest to my heart,
quickest on my tongue,
Gail Ann!

So far, our friendship's been about
church and singing—
church songs (of course),
but not only church songs,
also sweet songs,
like "Tonight You Belong to Me,"
by two sisters in California
named Patience and Prudence;
hillbilly songs,
like "Anytime,"
by Tennessee's own Eddy Arnold;
and silly songs,
like "How Much Is That Doggie in the Window?"
sung by Patti Page (and a barking dog).

Our friendship's been about sleepovers
at Gail Ann's grandmother's house on Hendrickson Street,
the mostly white neighborhood where she lives
with her mother, her sister, and her aunt Mattie Bell.
We eat
her grandma's blackberry jelly and apple butter,
and hear
Aunt Mattie Bell's conversations about politics.

But mostly,
we do each other's long hair,
plan our wardrobes for the next week,
talk and talk and talk,
listen to records,
and sing.

We talk about boys,
like Gail Ann's boyfriend,
who's in the Navy,
and about my own everlasting
crush on Robert Willis—
Oh Lord, why did I have to fall
for the preacher's son?

And now, our friendship will also be about
walking into Clinton High School together,
like we walked into Vine Junior High together,

like we walked into Austin High together.
Who knows, maybe together
we'll find new friends, but if not—
we'll still have each other,
one name among eight hundred
dearest to our hearts.

THE NIGHT BEFORE
(SUNDAY, AUGUST 26)

As I get ready the night before,
laying out what I will wear,
I'm thinking of first impressions—opening, closing the drawer.

Grandmother made me clothes I adore.
I make sure they are pressed. *Will anyone notice?* I wonder
as I get ready the night before.

A fresh new headband bought at the store
to match my blouse and skirt.
I'm thinking of first impressions—opening, closing the drawer.

Dad sharpens my pencils, then sharpens them more
with his knife, as he does every year. This, at least,
 can remain the same
as I get ready the night before.

Almost ready. There's one last chore:
Make a sandwich. I'll pack it for lunch.

I'm thinking of first impressions—opening, closing the drawer.

And then, at church, there's a prayer for peace,
but it sounds like we're going to war.
As I get ready the night before
I'm thinking of first impressions—
    please open, don't close, that door.

························· ☼ ·························

> **"Help us to love our enemies**
>   **and send our children down the hill**
>   **with peace in their hearts."**

—Prayer offered by Reverend O.W. Willis
at Mt. Sinai Baptist Church

PART 4

DOWN THE HILL
(LATE AUGUST TO LABOR DAY)

23

THE BALLAD OF THE HILL
(MONDAY, AUGUST 27)

We gather at our grammar school.
We bow our heads; we pray
that courage, kindness, and our faith
will shield us on this day.

Down the Hill we walk together,
boldness in our stride.
Eyes face forward, heads held up,
we're doing this with pride.

Chatting, joking, laughing—yes,
we keep our spirits high.
Along the road, some spectators—
just harmless passersby.

Now closer to the school we see
more spectators—with signs.
Our courage flags—how could it not?—
to read the chilly lines:

"We won't go to school with Negroes."
This marcher looks our age.
Is he a classmate? Where's he from?
Why should he feel outrage?

Two more pickets, two more signs,
but now I feel relief.
They're hurtful, but they're not a mob.
The pain is small and brief.

And now we're here; we mount the steps,
we enter this, our school.
We're safe. We're safe? Yes, safe inside,
where books, not pickets, rule.

We are the first in Tennessee
or any Southern state
to cause an all-white public school
to change—to integrate.

I can't help feeling prideful
(though pride's caused many to fall)
to know that I am one of twelve
to break this racial wall.

I can't help feeling hopeful
(though hope can trip and fall)

to know that I am one of twelve
to break
this
racial
wall.

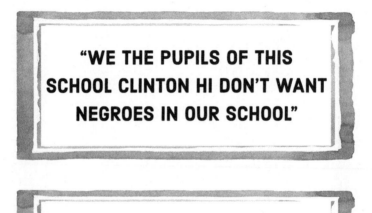

"WE THE PUPILS OF THIS
SCHOOL CLINTON HI DON'T WANT
NEGROES IN OUR SCHOOL"

"STRIKE AGAINST
INTEGRATION OF CLINTON HI"

—*Two more signs held by teenage
picketers on the first day of school*

"FIRST PUBLIC SCHOOL IN
OLD SOUTH INTEGRATED"

—Los Angeles Times, *August 28, 1956*

> ## "NEGRO PUPILS ENTER TENNESSEE SCHOOL"

—New York Times, *August 28, 1956*

> ## "CLINTON HIGH SCHOOL INTEGRATES RACES UNEVENTFULLY"

—Knoxville Journal, *August 28, 1956*

> ## "NEGRO STUDENTS ARE ADMITTED TO CLASSES AT TENNESSEE SCHOOL"

—Atlanta Daily World, *August 28, 1956*

24

INSIDE

Friendly faces:
Mrs. Anderson, the business teacher,
Mrs. Moser, the assistant principal,
Mrs. Brittain, who teaches home ec
and is the wife of Mr. Brittain,
the principal,
a skinny, serious-looking man,
but a friendly kind of serious.

Some of the white kids smile at me too.
A girl named Carol.
Who else, I can't tell you;
I don't have their names.
Tomorrow I'll learn more names.
Whoever smiles at me, I'll ask their names.

I think this is going to be fine.
I think this is going to be friendly,
but a serious kind of friendly
because in every class I am alone

in a sea of white,
the only Negro.

If school were weather, I would say it's serious
with a chance of friendly.

I meet up with Gail Ann and the others
briefly
where we make a tight little island in the hallway
before the tide pulls us apart
and we become driftwood again,
floating along, floating alone
in waters that we hope won't get too rough.

WHAT WILL BE

Home
never looked so good
   (tidy white frame),

never felt so fine
   (our living room, a pretty fresh green
   with its comfy sofa and armchairs,
   the piano for weekly lessons,
   the Victrola, the little table always
   set with flowers and framed photographs),

never seemed so safe
   (up on the Hill).

My bedroom shared with Mamie—
a sweet room, with red-robin-printed wallpaper,
a dressing table with frilly coverlet,
a closet full of clothes,
a two-story dollhouse on the floor—
a refuge.

Our front stoop—
sturdy cement, awning overhead—
a citadel.

The backyard fruit trees,
our own private Eden.

My father's biscuits,
manna from heaven.

My mother's chocolate pie,
ambrosia to sweeten the manna.

And the radio,
a big band at our fingertips
with Doris Day belting out her latest and greatest—
"Que Sera, Sera," the song is called,
or "Whatever Will Be, Will Be."
This white, blond, blue-eyed singer—
she is speaking directly to me
after a day that was hard but not horrible,
demanding but not dreadful.

I'll go back tomorrow.
Whatever will be, will be.

26

ME, MYSELF, BUT NOT COMPLETELY I
(TUESDAY, AUGUST 28)

Day Two.
The gathering.
The prayer.
The walk down the Hill.
A few more spectators along the route
who, I see, are not truly spectators.
They are protestors.
They have signs.
They are anti-integration.
They are anti-us.

Inside, smiles,
but also
glares.
Not more glares than smiles.
Still, glares are glares,
clouds rolling in on my
forecast.

And then . . . another change
in the weather,
refreshing
but also dangerous,
when Mrs. Davis calls me
to the front of the class,
and there I stand
before all my white classmates,
nervous
but not mortified
(what will be, will be).
Tell us about yourself, Jo Ann.
She invites them to ask me questions.

What are your favorite subjects?
I like biology. I like English.

What do you hope to be?
A doctor or a nurse.

What do you like to do in your spare time?
I like to read.

What are your favorite books?
I love *The Swiss Family Robinson.*
The Robe.
And *Black Beauty.*

What are your favorite movies?
Anything with Fred Astaire. Or John Wayne.
And musicals—
I loved *Oklahoma!*
And the Ma and Pa Kettle movies—
they always make me laugh out loud!

Where did you get those pretty clothes?
(I'm wearing my aqua pinstripe skirt and blouse.)
My grandmother—my mother's mother—made them for me.

Those are homemade clothes?
Yes, they are.
Grandmother Minnie is a very fine seamstress.

How many sets of clothes do you have?
Grandmother made me a whole new wardrobe
for school this fall.
She made me a different outfit
for every day of the week.
Tomorrow
I'll wear a different one.

The Jo Ann Allen Show ends
with another shift in the winds:
That smiling girl named Carol nominates me
to be vice president of our homeroom,

and this room full of white kids
elects me.

Mighty unpredictable
weather we're having.

"It's just that Jo Ann is so pretty and smart
and has such a wonderful personality. Anyhow, she had to be good to get elected; she
ran against a member of the football team."

—*Carol Peters, interviewed in*
New York Times Magazine,
September 16, 1956

27

LEFT UNSAID

What I left out of my answers
during the Jo Ann Allen Show . . .

on books:
I can't borrow *The Swiss Family Robinson*
or *Little Women*

or any other book I like
from Clinton's public library
because, as you know, the library is for white people—but

when I was eleven years old
and my favorites were fairy tales
(*Cinderella* and *Snow White*;
also anything by Hans Christian Andersen),
my dad had a job
cleaning the library.
I helped him
by washing the library floor.
Then I would sit at a table

and read books before we went home.
I mopped my way into fairy tales,
which, when you think about it,
sounds like a fairy tale.

On movies:
We watch the same ones,
you sitting anywhere you want,
according to your desire;
me sitting in the buzzard's roost,
according to my color.
Do our eyes fill with tears
in the same places?
Do we laugh
at the same lines?

About my grandmother the seamstress:
That's Grandmother Minnie,
light of skin,
whose own grandmother was a slave
brought to Tennessee
from somewhere,
I know not where.

Grandmother Minnie's husband,
Grandfather William,
also light of skin,

died when I was a little girl.
His own grandmother was also born into slavery,
owned (*quote unquote*)
by a family in Georgia
but brought somehow,
I know not how,
to Tennessee.

So my two great-great-grandmothers,
slaves,
had children with light complexions,
and narrow noses like yours (and mine),
and thin mouths like yours (and mine),
white enough to pass for white,
which means that
in the branches of my family tree
there are ancestors
who are as white
as you.

28

STORM BREWING
(WEDNESDAY, AUGUST 29)

Third day, Wednesday.
Gather.
Pray.
Walk.
Now the wind changes—
Taunts.
Screams.
Shock.

A crowd blocks the entrance.
We enter by the side.
Class is now a haven,
A place we can hide.

Noises outside rising.
Chants.
Slogans.
Fright.
Teachers want to teach:
Shut

Windows
Tight.

Hallways feeling different.
Glare.
Mutter.
Sneer.
But most kids kindly
Fend
Off
Fear.

Outdoor thunder rumbles—
The crowd's stormy voice.
Sheriff drives us home to safety.
Have
No
Choice.

Meeting after supper.
Gather.
Pray.
Talk.
Back to Knoxville? Sheriff asks.
No!
We
Shall
Walk.

WE WALK
(THURSDAY–FRIDAY, AUGUST 30–31)

The crowds grow larger,
Thursday, Friday,
waiting for us
as we make
our way
down the Hill
to our school.

Men, women, children, teenagers—
mothers holding chubby-cheeked babies—
line the street.
"Go back to Africa!"
"You'll never stay in school!"
are the nicer things
they holler.

I stop
packing a sandwich.

We all stop
going to the lunchroom.
It's just not comfortable.

And so, at lunchtime,
we walk,
me,
around the building in search of a quiet spot
to eat my apple,
finding Gail Ann if I can;
Alvah Jay with some of the other girls,
across the street to the jail
where her mother works as a cook;
Bobby, Maurice, Alfred, and Poochie,
over to the Richy Kreme stand
for hot dogs with mustard and chili
and maybe cones of frozen custard swirl.

Big mistake.
Protestors chase them
and attack them with sticks
and the signs they're carrying,
but it could've been worse.
Lucky the police come along
and break it up.
Bobby, Maurice, Alfred, and Poochie
can forget those hot dogs.

We walk down the Hill,
but we don't walk home,
because by afternoon
the crowd is large and rowdy
and we're driven up the Hill again in police cars.
Do I see George and Riley from across the street,
who have been to my house so many times,
whose mother borrows cups of sugar?
Have they really joined the mob?

All those cups of sugar.
All those cakes and pies
Mrs. Smith baked with those borrowed cups.
How did they bear to swallow them?
How do *I* bear
to swallow this?

"You and your people have been nicer to me
than my own relatives, but I just don't believe
in mixing of the races in school."

—*Mrs. Smith to Jo Ann's mother*, as quoted in
an Anti-Defamation League field report

30

HEARING/UNHEARING

"Don't pay attention,"
my dad says,
"to anything that's being said."
This is how he lives
with the insults,
spoken and unspoken,
that are part of our everyday lives.
This is how I live too,
or try to.

But you can't unhear
what you hear.
I can't unhear the time,
years ago,
when Dad took Mamie and me
into a little roadside store
to buy a few things.
A girl, five or six years old,
which was also Mamie's age then,
adorable as could be,

came out from behind the counter
where she and her mother were sitting:
"Oh, Mommy, look at the little nigger babies!"
Said it sweet as sugar.

That woman put her hand over
her little girl's mouth.
Dad put down
everything he was going to purchase.
"Let's go, girls," he said,
and we followed him as he walked out.

Don't pay attention to anything that's being said.
We walked out of that store.
We left behind that girl
with that word in her mouth,
a word that assaults us
almost daily.
But now, I don't want to walk out.
I want to walk in.
I can't unhear what I hear.
I won't walk away from it, either.

31

KASPER, NOT
THE FRIENDLY GHOST

Maybe
our white neighbors,
the ones we know and the ones we don't,
would have turned against us
anyhow.

Maybe
all the years of friendliness,
the sugar-borrowing and the joking with my father,
depended on us staying steadfastly
in our place
and out of their school.

Or maybe
they've been spooked by a ghost,
a ghost named Kasper.

John Kasper
is a stranger to Clinton,

a man from up North,
a young man
not so many years out of high school himself.

John Kasper
came to town last week
to tell white folks
that integration is un-American and un-Christian.

John Kasper
is minister of no church
but he preaches to the people
from the altar of racism,
knocking on doors in white neighborhoods,
showing those folks pictures
of Negro men and white women kissing
and saying that is what desegregation is about—

which is absolutely, positively
the worst possible thing
some people can imagine—

and he's in the courthouse square,
speechifying,
telling people they don't have to listen to the Supreme Court;
he's in front of school,
across the street from school,

down the street from school—
he's everywhere,
he's haunting Clinton,
he's a poltergeist
bringing forth the roar of the mob
the burning eyes
the contorted faces
the spitting
the hair-pulling
the tomato-throwing. . . .

Or maybe
John Kasper is no ghost.
He can't make anyone
do anything.
He leads,
people follow.
He speaks,
people listen.
He stirs up.
He spreads hatred.
People choose.

" 'Everything had been pretty quiet until he arrived,' the sheriff said. 'Now we've got a pretty ugly situation on our hands and we're going to have to have some help to maintain order.' "

—Knoxville Journal, *August 30, 1956*

"John Kasper, executive secretary of Seaboard White Citizens' Council . . . has been quoted in the Congressional Record (July 18, 1956) as stating the objectives of his organization to include the reversing of progress toward racial integration . . . and 'wiping out rock 'n' roll music.' "

—Knoxville Journal, *August 30, 1956*

"My classes are real nice and I believe everything would be all right if outsiders left us alone."

—*Jo Ann Allen to* Knoxville Journal, *August 31, 1956*

32

YOU ARE AS GOOD

When I see the hatred
When I hear the scorn
Of a town possessed
With its decency torn.

They would have me bend
But I stand up tall
I've got words inside
They can't make me crawl.

Don't pay attention,
my parents say.
You'll be somebody—
you will, someday.

If you show your fear,
then they will have won.
You are as good
as anyone.

You can be
whatever you want.
These words
These thoughts
This faith
Fight off every taunt.

33

PRINCIPAL BRITTAIN

When he decided
to enroll us in Clinton High School,
it wasn't out of any great love
for black people.
It wasn't out of any firm belief
in the righteousness of desegregation.
It was because
Judge Taylor said he had to.
He's made that clear.

But he's also made clear that,
though it took a court order
to drag him to our side,
now that he's here,
he is here.
Not *wobbly* here.
Strongly here.
He may not look
strongly
anything—
so wispy, a little bent,

shirt collar bigger than his neck,
and those giant glasses—
but he's not moving.

He gets phone calls at home,
one after another, all through the night,
people threatening him and Mrs. Brittain
for allowing us to attend school,
people hissing insults at them—
but he's not moving.

John Kasper and his followers
tell Mr. Brittain
that the parents of Clinton High students
want him to quit his job as principal—
but he's not moving.

John Kasper and his followers
tell Mr. Brittain
that the students of Clinton High School
want him to quit his job as principal—
but he's not moving.

Again and again
they tell him,
and he does not move,
again and again they say,

your students want you to quit,
and he doesn't wobble,

until he does . . .

. . . when he says he will leave
if fifty-one percent of the students want him to leave.

He calls a school assembly.
He puts in charge of the assembly
the captain of the football team,
who is also the student council president,
a tall boy with a crew cut named Jerry Shattuck,
and tells Jerry to have the students take a vote:
Should the principal stay or quit?
Mr. Brittain and all the teachers leave the auditorium.
The students of Clinton High School vote.

It's unanimous:
Mr. Brittain should stay.
When Mr. Brittain returns to the auditorium,
the kids clap and clap and clap.

Did he wobble?
Or did he know,
strongly,
that this is how our school can be?

34

MOB-CRAZY
(FRIDAY, AUGUST 31)

Outside the school auditorium
our nice, quiet, polite,
yes ma'am, no sir,
hat-tipping town

is going crazy.

Tonight
a crowd gathers at the courthouse square,
listening to speeches
on the evils of integration
and the wisdom of John Kasper.
John Kasper isn't there—
he's been arrested—
but his ideas, like a demon,
have taken possession
of a thousand people, maybe more,

who march through the streets shouting,

"We want Kasper!"
and who—some of them—
march to the mayor's house
and threaten to dynamite it,
and who—some of them—
set upon automobiles passing through Clinton,
the ones with Negro travelers,

those unlucky people
thinking they're just motoring through
on the way to their fun
Labor Day weekend plans,
no way to avoid trouble
because the highway runs through town,
becomes Main Street,
passes right by the courthouse square
a hop and a skip from our school—

and they end up in the middle of a riot,
angry white people rocking their cars.

Our nice, quiet, picture-pretty,
yes ma'am, no sir,
five-tower-bells-in-the-belfry courthouse
has gone mob-crazy.

35

TERROR
(SATURDAY, SEPTEMBER 1)

On this night,
the rabble returns to the courthouse square,
more speeches, more shouting,
anti- anti- anti- anti-
Kasper still in jail,
but that doesn't hinder
the two thousand people,
maybe three thousand,
crammed in the square.
There are plenty of others
to repeat his words
there in the shadow of the courthouse,
symbol of law, order, and
Brown v. Board of Education.

I'm not there to see this.
No Negro in his or her right mind
would be there.
But we hear what's going on.

Word spreads of the mobs,
and because there are no walls
to keep the mobs from rushing uphill
to our neighborhood,
we leave our home.
We go to our church,
where Mom and I, Mamie and Herbie
stay to sleep on the hard pews.
Better sore than sorry.

Dad and the other fathers—
I'm not sure where they are going;
maybe they will sit in the darkened houses,
maybe they will lie in a field,
maybe with guns
that are meant for hunting animals.

We pray out loud, together,
that we will be safe
and that this horror
will end.

36

JO ANN, GAIL ANN TIME
(SUNDAY MORNING, SEPTEMBER 2)

Since she doesn't live on the Hill,
Gail Ann didn't take shelter here in church last night
but she's here this morning.
No step-step game today.
All is serious.
And I want to know,
what was it like last night
on Hendrickson Street?

It was like this:
They sat in the dark house,
Gail Ann's uncles in the living room with shotguns,
her father down the road with a shotgun;
they heard a car behind the house near the shed,
her grandmother refused to be afraid,
and told Gail Ann's mother to put the outside spotlights on,
and nothing happened,

except Aunt Mattie Bell was so upset

watching the television coverage of our town
that she had to go throw up.

And now Gail Ann and I feel a rumble,
but not a stomach rumble.
This rumble we feel
under our feet.
This rumble
shakes the ground.
This rumble signals:
something's coming.

37

PEACEKEEPERS
(SUNDAY, NOON)

The tanks roll in at lunchtime,
a show of growling might,
as if in answer to the prayers
we prayed in fear last night.

Clinton's leaders asked for them;
the governor agreed.
They saw the lawless trampling
of the bigoted stampede.

The nights of wild rabble,
the faces warped with hate,
threats and curses, fevered speeches:
Segregate! Segregate!

So now the men in khaki clothes
patrol the streets and lanes.
Their bayoneted guns deter
the racists' harsh campaigns.

How strange to feel so comforted
by soldiers dressed for war,
but you would feel the same
if you had heard the mob's shrill roar.

Just let me go back to our school,
where English is my best,
where poems, stories, beauty, words
might blanket this unrest.

<hr />

"I am not doing this to promote integration or
segregation. I am doing this to promote law
and order, to preserve peace."

—*Statement of Tennessee Governor Frank Clement,
as reported in* Washington Post, *September 2, 1956*

38

TWO SIDES OF A COIN
(SUNDAY NIGHT)

Looking on the bright side,
it was our very own Mayor Lewallen
(who has always been against integration)
and our very own city council
(which has always been against integration)
who put out the call to Governor Clement
for help.

Looking on the bright side,
these white Clinton leaders
asked for soldiers
to stop the mob—
not to stop us.

Looking on the bright side,
the white governor of Tennessee sent in white soldiers
and thundering tanks
to protect our town—
not the white rabble-rousers.

That's the bright side.

Looking on the not-so-bright side,
someone,
or, probably, several someones,
set fire to a cross on the grounds
of Clinton High School.
That's Ku Klux Klan business,
and if anything is scarier than
John Kasper the poltergeist,
it's the KKK.

Looking on the not-so-bright side,
three thousand people have turned out tonight
at the courthouse square—
three thousand! our town doesn't even have four thousand!—
to holler (again) against integration.
We know
at least some of those three thousand
are not from Clinton,
but still.

Looking on the not-so-bright side,
a small mob
(if two hundred people are a small mob)
breaks off from the larger mob
when they notice a young black sailor

wearing his U.S. Navy blues and
walking toward the bus station.
They scream at him,
threaten him,
someone throws a bottle at him,
they could kill him.

Looking on the bright side,
the soldiers come to the rescue,
point their rifles at the horde
and help the sailor escape the mob,
so the mob can then resume its other important business,
such as throwing firecrackers at passing cars.

And looking on the bright side (again),
Gail Ann had a visit from her boyfriend, Grant, today,
James Grant Chandler:
the sailor
who came to town on a bus
wearing his Navy blues,
(carrying a present for Gail Ann—a radio!)
who was attacked
by that mob of white people
as he walked past the courthouse square
to catch the bus back to Knoxville.
He escaped,
thanks to the National Guard.

Bright side,
not-so-bright side.
If you flip the coin
that is Clinton tonight,
I think it will land on
its edge.

39

FIRST MONDAY
OF SEPTEMBER
(SEPTEMBER 3)

Labor Day:
a holiday
to honor those who work,
like my dad, who, but for the quirk
of bigotry could work
much more, much better
without the fetter
of racism that blocks him out
from jobs that white men get, and I don't doubt
that he could change some minds if they just knew
his personality—he's through-and-through
a man folks want to be around, and I have seen
him charm the white folks (lots of them)—he's got that keen
and clever conversation, that's my pops,
but when it comes to good work here in Clinton—

        all full stops.
        Jobs with mops.

And so my dad, he makes the drive up North
to Michigan; he travels back and forth
for work—to use his tools, to use his skill.
　　　　　He could complain.
　　　　　He never will.

40

DO THE MATH

Math is not my best or favorite subject,
but this arithmetic is elementary:

600 soldiers

+

100 jeeps and trucks

+

7 combat tanks

+

3 armored personnel carriers

+

1 helicopter

=

P lease, let the troops bring Clinton back from the
E dge of the cliff
A ll we want is to go to our school without the
C yclone of ugliness without fear without hate with
E ase.

600 soldiers

for a town
of not even 4,000
divided over
12 students:
I hope this is
a solvable equation.

41

A PROMISE

We have a special guest in our living room:
Major General Joe W. Henry,
State Adjutant General in Command
of the National Guard.

When he stands, he stands like a soldier.
When he sits, he sits like a soldier.
When he speaks,
you know he means what he says.

He tells us—
Mom and Dad and me and Mamie
and even Herbie—
that he and his soldiers are here
to protect us.
He promises they will stay

until we no longer need protection.

We feel reassured—

Mom and Dad and me and Mamie—
but Herbie, who's too young to understand much,
probably just feels awestruck
because there's a soldier
in the living room.

PART 5

TRY AGAIN
(THREE WEEKS
IN SEPTEMBER)

42

THIS TIME
(TUESDAY, SEPTEMBER 4)

By car, this time, we travel down the Hill
to face another day . . . another throng?
The streets are quiet, though, not harsh or shrill;
I hope—could be?—we all might get along.
Inside our school, the halls are far from full;
So many students absent; do they feel
afraid, like us, of trouble—or the pull
of trouble, hate, and segregation's zeal?
Three thirty comes, and so I find my friends
to gather once again to face the world.
The noise—*oh!*—not mobs, but men with pens,
reporters asking how our day unfurled.
    And then we walk, my friends and I;
      our laughing, teasing, jokes—our battle cry.

"They were brought to school in cars. However, when the session ended at 3:30 P.M. (4:30 New York time) seven of them walked home swinging their books and chatting gayly up the steep hill leading to the Negro settlement some 2,000 yards away."

—New York Times, *September 5, 1956*

43

COME BACK!
(WEDNESDAY, SEPTEMBER 5)

There is no danger involved at all

* * *

Your children will be provided protection

Dear Parent,

If your child has not been attending High School may we make this appeal to you to send your child back to school?

. . . .

We are no longer faced with the problem of integration vs. segregation. That has been decided for us by the highest courts in our land. Our problem now lies within our own minds and hearts. Your emotions may cry out against integration, but your mind tells you that you are a law abiding citizen, and your heart warns you against doing your child an injustice by hindering his education. The way of wisdom is the way of constructive thinking and loving hearts.

*—Notice sent home from the Clinton High School
Parent-Teacher Association Executive Committee*

It's quiet
inside a building
that can hold eight hundred
when only three hundred
show up.
Quiet.
Relief.

Come back!
the school pleads
with the five hundred
who aren't here.
Come back!

If it were
Negro students
who stayed home
or found another school
(back on the bus to Knoxville),
would we hear
Come back?
Or would we hear
Quiet.
Relief
that we'd disappeared?

44

WE ARE THE NEWS

> **"AGITATOR FIGHTS U.S. ORDER HERE: INFLUENCES PEOPLE TO DEFY LAW, THREATENS SCHOOL STUDENTS"**
>
> —Clinton Courier-News, *August 30, 1956*

> **"FIGHTS AGAIN MAR INTEGRATION STEP"**
> "Apples and tomatoes were hurled at a Negro woman in today's disturbance. . . ."
>
> —New York Times, *August 31, 1956*

> **"UNRULY MOB TAKES OVER IN CLINTON"**
>
> —Knoxville Journal, *September 1, 1956*

The news is something
that happens
to other people
in other places.

Until it happens to you.

We are the news,
here.
We are the news,
everywhere.

> ## "TANK–LED NATIONAL GUARD QUIETS TOWN IN TENNESSEE"

—New York Times, *September 3, 1956*

> ## "NEGROES OF CLINTON MUM"
>
> "Stoic determination and frightened silence were the prevailing attitudes today on 'Foley Hill,' the Negro settlement in Clinton."

—Washington Post, *September 4, 1956*

> ## "TROOPS CLEAR STREETS IN DESEGREGATION ROW"

—Los Angeles Times, *September 4, 1956*

> ## "TENNESSEE INTEGRATION GOES ON DESPITE RIOTS"

Washington Post, *September 5, 1956*

> ## "GUARD HERE HAS 600 MEN, 100 VEHICLES"

—Clinton Courier-News, *September 6, 1956*

The president of the United States is someone
who makes speeches about
other people
in other places.

Until he makes a speech about you.

.... ✦ ....

**"It is difficult through law and through force
to change a man's heart."**

*—President Dwight D. Eisenhower,
September 5, 1956, talking about violence
breaking out because of school integration*

We are the news,
here.
We are the news,
everywhere.
In New York City.
In Washington, DC.
Baltimore, Maryland.
Los Angeles, California.
Chicago, Illinois.
Detroit, Michigan.
Japan. Yes, Japan!

My parents collect
the newspaper and magazine reports.
Sometimes I don't recognize
the place
these articles describe.
Like when they talk about
"the Negro settlement" in Clinton.
Negro *settlement?*
We are not the Jamestown colonists.
Or when they talk about the
"shacks"
in our neighborhood.

We have homes here,
some nice, some not-so-nice,

some brick, some frame, some cinder block.
We are not a neighborhood of shacks.

But other times I recognize
this place and its people
completely.

Like when the newspaper quotes my mother,
"Mrs. Herbie Allen,"
answering the reporter's question
about whether her daughter—
me—
would be returning to school
after the Labor Day weekend riots:
"It's the Sabbath and I've been to church
to pray and seek consolation.
I found my consolation there
and don't want to talk to anyone today."

Yes, that is my mom.

And when the newspaper quotes my father:
"Those instigating the scenes at Clinton High
are wrong in their way of thinking.
We are down there because
the Supreme Court has said
that's where our children are going to school.

I'm not sending Jo Ann to school
to marry white boys.
We want her to get an education."

Yes, that is my pops.

And when President Eisenhower said,
"It is difficult through law and through force
to change a man's heart"—
Yes, that is Clinton.

Yes, it is difficult
to change a promise of change
into real change

and that is news
to no one.

45

SPEAKING OF
PRESIDENT EISENHOWER

I remember four years ago,
my parents, excited to vote
for General Dwight D. Eisenhower,
hero of the Second World War,
to be president of the United States—
"I Like Ike!" was the slogan—
my dad telling everyone,
"We have to vote!"

and they voted.
My dad drove old Mrs. Shockley from across the street
to the voting place
and the other elderly folks in the neighborhood too,
because
"We have to vote!"

and they went in his shiny black Buick
and voted.

General Eisenhower won the election,
became President Eisenhower,
and my parents were happy.

But now, they feel let down.
I know a president has big things
to take care of,
like keeping us out of war,
or winning wars,
like worrying about the Soviet Union
and Communism
and the Suez Canal crisis
and strikes at steel mills
and building highways all over the country
but,
my parents say,
you, President Eisenhower,
haven't come out strongly
for school desegregation.

Yes, Mr. President,
"It is difficult through law and through force
to change a man's heart,"
but when a reporter asked you if you supported
Brown v. Board of Education
you answered:

"I think it makes no difference
whether or not I endorse it.
What I say is,
the Constitution is as the Supreme Court interprets it;
and I must conform to that
and do my very best to see
that it is carried out
in this country."

Yes, yes.
That is what the leading citizens of Clinton say.
The law of the land.
The Supreme Court has ruled.
We are law-abiding people.
But what if you said:
Brown v. Board is right!
Brown v. Board is just!
Brown v. Board is the American way!
What if you said:
I like *Brown v. Board*!

Then, I think, my parents would still be saying
I Like Ike.

46

THE MAYOR

Like the president,
like the principal,
like the P-TA,

the mayor is lukewarm
on integration.

He's written a "statement"—
"First, let me say that
Clinton is a 'southern' town,
true to the traditions, love,
and respect of the Southland."

I know he doesn't think
schools with black and white children
are part of those Southland "traditions."

He continues:
"The present emergency,
which today finds its focal point in Clinton,

is a national problem brought about
by the decision of
the United States Supreme Court
in ordering integration
of the public school system."

And don't forget,
"We in Clinton and Anderson County
did not seek to allow Negroes
to enter the public schools.
In fact, we have for five years
actively fought in the Federal Court
to prevent this happening."

Yes, "We in Clinton and Anderson County"
fought Alvah Jay's mom,
whose lawsuit for Alvah's sister Joheather
went on so long, what with all that active fighting,
that Joheather was done with school
by the time the Supreme Court said
segregation was wrong
and Judge Taylor said Alvah Jay's mom
was right.

To conclude,
"The people of Anderson County will, I know,
even though the decision of the Supreme Court is

'a bitter dose,'
obey the law."

Lukewarm.
But law-abiding.
That puts Mayor Lewallen on our side.
With friends who call you "a bitter dose,"
who needs enemies?

DAY BY DAY
(MONDAY, SEPTEMBER 10)

With every passing day
more white kids return to school.

With every passing day
more people return to Clinton's streets,
not to yell and spit,
but to shop,
to nod politely,
to talk neighborly.

With every passing day
I like to think
maybe all this good behavior
isn't because there are six hundred soldiers
patrolling our town, but rather because
people really are kind, not hateful.

But with every passing day
I have to think

that all the good behavior
cannot be disconnected from the six hundred soldiers
because if I feel
comforted,
mustn't those people who were
yelling and spitting,
and those boys with their nasty signs,
and those men who attacked Gail Ann's boyfriend,
mustn't they feel
discomforted,

and how long will they stand for that?

With every passing day
I am grateful for the kids in school
who are kind, not hateful,
but even so,
when I look in their faces,
I see there will no longer be
new friends
in my forecast.

" 'They (the Negroes) have got to have an education like everyone else,' said a 13-year-old freshman girl with a pretty smile and sparkling eyes. 'I don't think there's any of us who really wanted to go to school with Negroes—but now that they're here, we might as well make the best of it.'

"Another white girl, 16 and a senior, agreed in substance, but added: 'I think it's all right as long as there are only 12 of them, but if more come in—and you know there will be more—I think the county ought to build a high school for them.' "

—*"Clinton Students Themselves Find Middle Ground On Integration,"* Knoxville Journal, *September 9, 1956*

48

GONE
(TUESDAY, SEPTEMBER 11)

Gone are the screamers
Gone are the crowds
Gone is the thunder
of angry white clouds.

Calm are the classrooms
Calm are the halls
Calm are the streets
(mostly)
Calmed are the brawls.

Decency rises
Decency won
Decency spurred
by a soldier, a gun.

Clinton is quiet
Clinton is still
Order in town

Calm on our Hill.

Soldiers are leaving
Trucks rumbling out
The job here is done
(they say)
I know those who doubt.

Gone are the soldiers
Gone are the tanks
Gone is the general
To whom we owe thanks.

Gone is protection
Gone is the shield
Gone.
Will our neighbors' true hearts be revealed?

"As the last three armored personnel carriers of the National Guard rumbled away from Clinton, which has taken on its former little-town atmosphere of peace and stillness, sixty-one more students who had stayed at home during the two-week disturbances entered the school."

—Washington Post, *September 12, 1956*

"I feel sure we will have violence once the guards are removed."

—Reverend O.W. Willis, pastor of Mt. Sinai Baptist Church, in Baltimore Afro-American, September 15, 1956

49

ALSO GONE:
LULA T. SHOCKLEY, 1892–1956
(SATURDAY–SUNDAY, SEPTEMBER 15–16)

"Mother Lula" is what we call Mrs. Shockley
from across the street
because when we were younger
she took care of us,
Mamie and me,
at her big, beautiful house
when our parents had to be at work.
I loved going there,
with its fancy furniture
and beautiful things
and long screened porch out back

and Mother Lula herself,
who never minded us touching
her delicate bric-a-brac,
who made us food we didn't get at home

like frog legs that danced in the skillet

when she cooked them with salt,
because that is what frog legs do,
and who served tomatoes
sprinkled with sugar,
who put mustard plasters around our necks
if we started to get sick.

It's Mother Lula who's been sick,
with cancer.
We know she is nearing the end,
we know this weekend is her last on Earth,
and so we sit
in her beautiful living room
while Mother Lula is across the hall
in her bedroom
with her family,
getting ready to pass.
This is how we do it,
we sit and wait and talk in low voices
about the person whose time has come,
so a body doesn't have to die alone,
so those who love her can feel
not only sorrow but also comfort
and company.

Saturday is my birthday,
but I'm not a child anymore,

and if I have to sit in Mother Lula's house
waiting for her to pass,
I do not mind. I want to.
She has been a good friend to us.
She's been like a grandmother.
She's worried about us like we were her own.
So here we are in her house this weekend,
until on Sunday
Mother Lula passes
and I am now a fifteen-year-old.

50

A NICE WALK

Some days,
Bobby Cain and I walk home from school together
to Jarnigan Street,
437 for me, 434 for him.
We set out, talking about the day.
Was it a better day than yesterday?
Was it worse?
Either way, it's a nice walk.

I know that Bobby wanted to keep going
to Austin High in Knoxville,
to have this year, his senior year, at a place
that was familiar and friendly to him,
even if it was a long ride away,
but the desegregation order came down,
and Clinton High became his school.
It's hard for him,
harder for him than for me and the others,
because the people who hate
that we're in classes with students

at Clinton High School
hate even more
the idea of a Negro student graduating
with the white students.

So Bobby gets more of the bad—
name-calling, threats, shoving, spitting.
I know he thought of quitting
during those first few days,
but if the people who attacked him
in the ruckus at the Richy Kreme
thought they would scare him away,
they were wrong.
Since then he is like a rock,
not only still here,
but solid and strong and determined,
a hero in the making,
not that I would say that to him.
He would think I was exaggerating
or teasing
or, maybe, flirting,
and I am not flirting with Bobby Cain.
I am listening to his soft talk
of his hard days
on our nice walk.

51

WHAT A WHIRLWIND IS
(SATURDAY, SEPTEMBER 22)

Dizzying,
to take off, Carol Peters and her mother and I,
on an airplane bound for Washington, DC;

daunting,
to know that the world is watching Clinton
and will soon be watching us
when we appear before cameras.

To think that Mrs. Anderson or Mrs. Davis
or maybe a news reporter—
whoever it was—
suggested that Carol and I go
on television!

To think that my parents agreed!

It's a bumpy flight,
so rough and stormy that I—

oh, mortification!—
get sick.

It's not as if I haven't flown
on an airplane before.
When I was eight years old,
I flew to California with
my aunt Mamie Lou
for a visit with my uncle Samuel.
That didn't make me sick at all.
The trip back to Tennessee,
that was another matter.
We took a train—
that's a *lo-oo-ng* train ride—
and part of the way through,
we had to move
from where we were comfortably sitting
to the "colored car,"
which was not as nice.
That was a little bit sickening.

But now, on the airplane to Washington,
the stewardess in charge
is kind to me.
She puts me up in a first-class seat
for a while
to help me feel better,

and it does make parts of me feel better,
although not necessarily my stomach.

Strange and surprising,
to say good-bye to Carol and Mrs. Peters
for the night.
They go to lodging for white people,
where I may not stay.
Of course: segregation is here in the nation's capital.

I am taken to the YWCA.
The lady in charge, a Negro lady, is nice.
The Y is clean, also
a little terrifying,
since there is *no one* else staying here at the Y, also
a little thrilling,
since there is *no one* else staying here at the Y!

Can a person be
terrified
yet
thrilled
at the same time?
I can answer that.
Yes.
That is what a whirlwind is.

52

IN THE STUDIO
(SUNDAY, SEPTEMBER 23)

We are here, Carol and I,
to be the black and white faces
on the black-and-white screen,
to interview—
drum roll, please!—
the Attorney General of the United States
about the problems of school desegregation.

Yes—we! teenagers from little Clinton, Tennessee.
And he—Herbert Brownell Jr.—
the highest law enforcement officer
in the United States government,
a man who gives President Eisenhower advice,
a man who is in charge of
all the lawyers in the government,
a man who makes sure the Constitution
is enforced,
and who is probably on television all the time.

The television show:
College Press Conference,
where students are invited
to ask questions of
important people about
important issues.
We're not college students,
obviously,
but here we are, anyway,
sitting at a round table
with microphones and cameras and lights
and the Attorney General of the United States,
who acts like these microphones and cameras and lights
are nothing special,
while I am just about to pass out from excitement.

53

FACING THE CAMERAS

My heart's

pounding
pounding
pounding

Will I freeze, will I go weak?

Pound pound pounding

My turn.
I speak.

LEFT UNSAID, AGAIN

I don't faint away,
but I don't say what I came to say.
I don't ask the questions
that I wrote down,
that, if I'm being honest,
my uncle Samuel in California
wrote down for me in a letter.

They are good questions.
They aren't easy questions.
The people who run the program
don't like the questions I came with.
They ask me—
tell me—
not to ask them.
So I don't.
I ask easy questions.
Attorney General Brownell gives easy answers.

> "Jo Ann asked Mr. Brownell if the President plans to make a speech on civil rights during the presidential campaign.
>
> "'I don't know,' he answered. 'But I plan to make one.'"

That was the best I could do?

I spoke.
But I also froze.
I didn't say what I came to say.

55

SPEAKING OUT

Off-camera,
I have a second chance.

Now it's our turn to be interviewed
by a writer for the *Baltimore Afro-American* newspaper.
Without the glare
of the lights,
without the supervision
of the bigwigs,
without the
pound pound pounding
my words are easier,
more natural,
more me
(and Uncle Samuel).

Me:
"President Eisenhower should use his authority
  to help integrate schools in the South."

Carol:

"Integration should be a minor problem.

I don't think it will take Tennessee more than two years

to integrate all of its schools."

Me (smiling):

"It shouldn't take that long."

Me:

"President Eisenhower should have more to say

about the situation."

I don't think I'm still smiling,

and I feel fine.

56

WHAT'S OVER
(TUESDAY, SEPTEMBER 25)

Summer is over.
My big trip is over.
A month of school is over.

In our front yard, leaves on the giant sycamore tree
start their transformation
into giant brown hands that will let go next month.
In our giant backyard, leaves on the little plum trees,
stubbornly, steadfastly stay
purple purple purple,
until they finally give up.
The honeysuckle that clutches our back fence,
giving us sweet nectar and that delicious scent,
loosens its grip,
soon to shrivel and disappear.
Over, over, over.

Maybe thinking about all *that*—
all that

segregation, integration, law, courts,
rights, prejudice, demonstrators—
will be over too.

I want to
and I will
watch Saturday morning television with Mamie,
play jacks with her
and tiddlywinks and pick-up sticks
and Chinese checkers and marbles.

I want to
and I will
play Old Maid with my family,
and Scrabble and Candyland too,
and watch *The Ed Sullivan Show* on Sunday night
and eat up every last crumb of corn bread at dinner.

I want to
and I will
sing at church,
sing for fun,
shake hands with the sycamore leaves,
suck the juice from the last plums,
say good-bye to the honeysuckle,
not thinking too hard about what's over,
not wondering too much about what's next.

PART 6

FEAR
(LATE SEPTEMBER TO MID-NOVEMBER)

57

BOOM
(WEDNESDAY, SEPTEMBER 26)

When word comes
the Ku Klux Klan
is driving up the Hill,
my father gets his gun.
We live here.
He won't run.

When word comes
the KKK
is driving down our streets,
my father steps outside.
We live here.
He won't hide.

When noises *BOOM!*
CRACK-CRACK! POP-POP!
Stay here, my father says.
He runs to find the cause.

We live here.
He won't pause.

The word comes back:
dynamite.
Terror in the night.
This bomb is Ku Klux white.
We live here.
Do we fight?

When word comes
my dad's in jail—
my dad! And not the bombers!
His crime? There's only one:
A black man
with a gun.

"Officers said that if the explosion was calculated to throw fear into the Negro residents of Clinton, it was successful. A number armed themselves fearing another such incident and one man, Herbert Allen, who lives on Jarnigan Street, some distance from the scene of the explosion was arrested by Sheriff Woodward for carrying arms. The sheriff said Allen's .38 caliber revolver had never been fired."

—The Oak Ridger, *September 27, 1956*

58

RULES FOR LIFE

Just as there are rules
for shopping in Clinton—
Negroes may buy things at the drugstore
but may not sit at the lunch counter there,
Negroes must wait
before entering the grocery aisle
until the white customer exits,
Negroes must put scarves on their heads
before trying on a hat;

just as there are rules
for working in Clinton—
Negroes may work
as janitors and maids,
car washers and dishwashers,
but not in good jobs
at the hosiery mill
or the cannery
or in shops or offices;

there are rules
for living in Clinton.
Here is one known to all:
No Negroes with guns.

Of course, everyone knows that we,
like white people,
have hunting guns.
Every family has a hunting gun.
That is not against the rules.
But my father wasn't hunting
the night he got arrested.
It wasn't a hunting gun
the sheriff saw.
My father was defending us.
He was defending our neighborhood,
and that is not something a Negro can do
with a gun in his hands
here in Clinton,
maybe not anywhere.

So Pops was arrested.
So he went to jail.

But not for long.

59

HOW IT WORKS

My mother calls Mrs. Crenshaw,
who talks to Mr. Crenshaw,
who runs Magnet Mills here in Clinton,
who likes my dad
(but won't hire him at the mill
because of those rules),
and who talks to someone,
who talks to someone,
and my father is released from jail,
home,
only a few hours later.

Those kids at my elementary school
used to tease me
because of the way I talk and behave—
"You think you're Mrs. Crenshaw!"
Maybe some of them knew
that part of my name,
the *Ann* of Jo Ann,
is for the Crenshaws' daughter.

Mrs. Crenshaw and Ann love my mother
and knew her way back
when she was pregnant with me.
Ann Crenshaw asked my mother
to name her baby after her,
so she did, partway.

But no, I would never make the mistake
of thinking that I'm Mrs. Crenshaw or Ann Crenshaw
or Mr. Crenshaw or any white person.
Look at how they can make things happen
just with a telephone call.
Look at how,
with all that love the Crenshaws have for my mother,
with all the good feeling they have toward my family,
my father does not have a job at the mill, and
the Crenshaws do not speak out
in favor of the desegregation of Clinton High School.
They do not break the rules for living in Clinton,
and neither—mostly—do we.

60

WHO DID IT
(SATURDAY, OCTOBER 13)

We said
it was the KKK.
They said
the bombers got away.
We said
IT WAS THE KKK!
We feared

they'd come another day.

We're right.
It happens Saturday night.
Hundreds
of people hooded in white.
Burning
four crosses, their sick rite.
Cruising
our Hill. But we sit tight.

They say
it was the KKK.
We say
we know.
And the terrors replay.

--------------- ✦ ---------------

"Clinton was the scene of another segregationist meeting Saturday night attended by 125
carloads of hooded Ku Klux Klan members."

—The Oak Ridger, *October 15, 1956*

"Newsmen were chased from the scene, but
one speaker was heard on a public address
system referring to 'The nine devils on the
Supreme Court.'"

—Washington Post, *October 16, 1956*

THE LITTLE THINGS

It's the little things that help.
A kind smile from Carol Peters,
an encouraging talk with Mrs. Moser,
a compliment from Mrs. Anderson.

The smile sweet as nectar,
the talk so caring,
the compliment, genuine.
Gold, not dross,
light, not gloom,
virtue, not vice.

It's the little things that hurt.
A spitball at the back of your neck,
a shove in the hallway,
curses when you walk to class.

The spitball when the teacher's not looking,
the shove not hard enough to knock you over,
the curses muttered.

Ripples, not waves,
gnats, not wasps,
thorns, not chains.

When I lay them out like this,
Helpful Little Things v. Hurtful Little Things,
they look like they balance out,
but when I weigh them on my scale of pain—
they don't.

THE NECESSARY THINGS

The few words
exchanged
in the hallway
between classes.
   You all right?
   Everything okay?
   Keep your head up!
We've known each other
since Green McAdoo
so we don't need a lot
but
if we are going to get through the day
without feeling completely alone—
those few words
those stolen seconds
those familiar faces
are necessary.

THE LOST THINGS

If you wear a pretty dress,
like Anna Theresser's dress
of yellow and blue and white fabric
that *anybody* would have to admire;

and if you go through the day
without encountering Mrs. Anderson,
who would be sure to notice it,
sure to tell you how lovely you look;

and if the rest of us don't see you,
because you are a freshman
and most of us are older,
and because you don't live on the Hill,
and because you didn't go to Green McAdoo
except for a few months when you were thirteen—

does your dress lose its prettiness?

And have we lost something good—

some tenderness, some kindliness—
by being so intent on getting through
our days
ourselves
unscathed
that we have not seen, really seen, this dress?

There is a newspaper photo
with Anna Theresser, wearing her dress
of yellow and blue and white,
but, as in all newspaper photos,
the colors are lost.
It's black and white.

AND THEN THERE ARE THE THUMBTACKS

Scattered on our chairs
A prank straight out of cartoons
They think we don't look?

65

LUNCHTIME

Me, in a quiet corner
of an empty classroom,
munching an apple, if I brought one.
I'll eat at home, after school.

Gail, in study hall. She'll eat after school too.
She might come to my house then
and eat an onion sandwich—
bread,
    onion sliced thick,
       mayonnaise—
while I look on and say,
"Not even a tomato slice?!"
No. This is how she likes it.

Anna Theresser, at a lunchroom table
near the teachers
because teachers are safe.

Alvah Jay, with her mother across the street

at the jail,
or, sometimes, with Anna Theresser
near the teachers.

The others,
I don't know.
I don't see them.

What I know is that
lunchtime isn't lunchtime.
It's not social hour.
It's not recess.
Lunchtime sets students free,
and I fear those freed white students
now more than ever.
I fear what they might do to me
outside the classroom and
unseen by teachers.
Unpredictable and full of peril,
lunchtime isn't lunchtime,
and the sooner I'm done
not eating
and back in a classroom,
the better.

THE KLAN, AGAIN
(WEDNESDAY, OCTOBER 24)

What type of people
set out to burn a cross
in the front yard of
a teacher?

People in white masks
wearing white robes:
cowards.

"Mrs. Celadon Lewallen, Eagle Bend Road,
thwarted an attempt to burn a cross in front
of her home about 9 p.m., but one was burned
about half an hour later in front of Mrs. Elea-
nor Davis's home on South Main St."

—Clinton Courier-News, *October 25, 1956*

"INCIDENTS"
(THURSDAY, NOVEMBER 8)

> ### "SHOTS FIRED AT NEGRO HOME HERE"
>
> "This is the latest of a series of 'incidents' including a
> dynamiting, rock throwing, threatening telephone calls,
> and other forms of harassment to which negro families
> have been subjected since Clinton High School has been
> integrated and which have been reported to police."

—Clinton Courier-News, *November 8, 1956*

When there's one "incident" after another
following us up the Hill,
how can we ever be at peace?

You can't call the police every time,
not for the vicious phone calls, not
when there's one "incident" after another.

Shots fired last night at the Williams house,
that brought the police, investigating who's
following us up the Hill.

But the white neighbor boys banging on our house,
terrorizing us—they don't follow us, they live here.
How can we ever be at peace?

68

THEIR SILENCE

Our school
is smaller.
White kids came back
after the upset
of the first weeks.
But not all came back.

Maybe their parents were afraid
for them,
or couldn't stand
the idea of them mixing
with us.

They might have asked me.
I could have assured them:
there is no mixing.

That Jo Ann Allen Show
in my homeroom back in August,
that was about it for me.

That vice presidency vanished.
That connection with Carol Peters
weakened week by week.

Even if our smaller school
has shed itself of the worst haters
who can't stand to breathe
the same air as us,
it is full of white kids
who look through us, speak around us,
wall us off with indifference;
and those who started out friendly
have pulled back.

Principal Brittain may have asked
the football team—the Clinton Dragons—
to keep the halls peaceful,
to look out for us,
and maybe they do
(I don't see them),
but he can't make them
make friends with us.

And so I go through the school day
surrounded by a hard shell of silence,
chitchat and cheer bouncing off the walls,
none of it meant for me.

69

OUR SILENCE

We make our own silence too.
When a group of us
is walking down the Hill,
we don't talk about
why we are walking down the Hill
and why we may end up in a police car
back up the Hill
for our own protection
when our school day ends.

When Gail Ann and I get together
after school,
we are not talking about
the biggest thing happening in our lives.

Silence.
Not the stony kind,
but the stoic kind,
the silence that says
we've said what we need to,

we'll carry on,
let's talk about something else.
Anything else.

Silence can say a lot, though.
Gail Ann's silence
about what is happening
makes the anger I see in her face, her eyes,
and the set of her jaw,
loud and clear;
her anger about the word *colored*,
new and defiant;
her anger that fends off fear,
fearsome.

70

IN THE GARDEN, 1

Sometimes when I walk
or when I sit
and it feels too hard,
what we're doing feels like a burden,
so heavy,
too much—
the song Mamie and I sang at Easter
comes to me.

> *He speaks, and the sound of His voice*
> *Is so sweet the birds hush their singing*
> *And the melody,*
> *That He gave to me;*
> *Within my heart is ringing.*

> *And He walks with me, and He talks with me,*
> *And He tells me I am His own;*
> *And the joy we share as we tarry there,*
> *None other has ever known.*

I'd stay in the garden with Him,
Tho' the night around me be falling,
But He bids me go;
Through the voice of woe,
His voice to me is calling.

The kids who yank my ponytail,
shove me in the hall,
trip me,
send spitballs flying at me—
as if they have a God-given right to fling
hands, feet, spit my way!—
they don't matter
when I think of being in the garden.
And the burden feels less heavy.

IN THE GARDEN, 2

Sometimes when we walk
down the Hill,
toward the railroad tracks,
headed to school,
a lady is outside
in her garden.
Looks like she's digging up weeds,
but she takes that spade
and she flips dirt at us.
Dirt!
We are planting ourselves
in Clinton High School,
and she can't pluck us out like weeds.
She sure can show us, though,
this is not how she thinks a garden should grow.

CALIFORNIA CALLING

Uncle Samuel says,
Come to California!
Here, there's work equal to Herbert's skills and smarts.
Here, Jo Ann can finish high school in peace.
Here, Mamie and little Herbie will never
go through what Jo Ann is going through.
Our schools are already integrated.
People are used to it,
unlike in the South.
Come to California!
Live in Los Angeles!
Get out of the South!

Uncle Samuel left Tennessee long ago,
left everything about it behind,
it seems to me.
Even his last name—
he and Mom and Aunt Mamie Lou were born Hoppers—
he changed to Harper
and never looked back.

He went to the Tuskegee Institute,
was a Tuskegee airman during the war,
married Aunt Amanda, and had three kids.
He moved to Los Angeles,
where he and Aunt Amanda are teachers,
and where he says we should move—*now*.

Come to California!
Uncle Samuel says to my mother, his sister.
I believe she is tempted, but
I'm stubborn, my father says.
And Jo Ann is stubborn.
She wants to finish what she started.
I do?
I do. Of course I do.
Uncle Samuel has to understand.
He's a Tuskegee airman.
Spit Fire
is the Tuskegee motto.
Sounds fierce;
I'm not.
But I am stubborn.
Spit Fire stubborn.
I want to stay right here.

73

OUT THERE
(TUESDAY, NOVEMBER 13)

Not *all* news happens here.

Out there, on this day,
there's a brand-new Supreme Court ruling:
race segregation on buses is unconstitutional!
Is this the end of going to the back of the bus
on our shopping trips to Knoxville?
I think so!
Is this the end of the ditty we all know and despise?

If you're white, you're right.
If you're brown, stick around.
If you're black, get back.
I think not. Probably not the end of that.

Out there: Elvis Presley
on *The Ed Sullivan Show*!
Oh, but that news was very much here, too,
here, where we watched him,

Mom, Grandmother Minnie, Aunt Mamie Lou,
me and Mamie and our four little cousins,
all of us dancing and cutting up and singing
and imitating that gyrating thing he does—historic!
Is this the beginning of dance parties
where my King's-English mother
and my be-a-lady grandmother
swing their hips
to the bop-bop-bop of "Don't Be Cruel"?
No. Probably not the beginning of that.

And way out there,
students in a country called Hungary
are protesting their government
controlled by the Soviet Union,
workers and others joining in,
marching for freedom, fighting for freedom, and then—
in roll the tanks from the Soviet Union.
In march the soldiers from the Soviet Union.
Freedom crushed.
I think of the tanks that rolled into Clinton.
I think of the soldiers.
Freedom upheld.

These things going on at the same time,
tanks and soldiers oppressing,
tanks and soldiers uplifting.

What a big world it is.

What a lot of struggle.

Mustn't forget the good news.

Like seats in the front of the bus.

Like Elvis.

PART 7

GOING DOWNHILL
(MID-NOVEMBER TO DECEMBER)

74

THE BIG THINGS

It's the big things
that grow from the little things:

The little shoves
that become
the shove that almost knocks Gail Ann out the window
from the second floor of the school building.

The little paper spitballs
that become
paper notes with obscene messages
that become
a bathroom wall painted with **"Coon. Go home."**

The muttered comments
that become
KEEP WHITE SCHOOLS WHITE
on big bold buttons
worn by girls and boys right here in school
who call themselves the

"Tennessee White Youth,"
inspired by John Kasper,
now out of jail.

Where once they kept their distance,
the white kids who hate us
are up close now, hard on our heels,
truly stepping on our heels—
Gail Ann's are bloody.

From the little slights
come the larger evils,
and they feel

monstrous.

75

AT NIGHT

In our room
Mamie and I say prayers
before bed
on our knees
on the floor.
Lord Jesus,
I pray,
please keep me safe
and my friends safe
and not let anyone harm us.
We say *Amen,*
and Mamie says her prayer,
which is a lot like mine.
Some nights we cry a little,
because even believers
can be afraid.

AROUND TOWN

I don't need chocolate enough
to want to go into Hoskins to buy a candy bar
and feel the stares
when I'm just trying to be a customer.

I don't want movies enough
to need to go to the Ritz Theatre
and feel the eyes on me
when I enter the door to the buzzard's roost.

I don't need
I don't want
I don't care
to walk around Clinton
as if it's still our town,
and be reminded that,
in many ways,
it's not.
It's hostile territory,
not crazed by the mob,

but tainted by everyday meanness.

If claiming our rights
could so easily unleash these wrongs,
maybe it was never our town at all.

CLOSING IN

When Gail Ann hears a white girl tell a teacher
that she and her friends were misbehaving because
"we don't want to go to school with these niggers,"
and the teacher responds,
"I feel the same as you do, but honey, we have to do it"—

When Regina sits in study hall
surrounded by 150 white kids, and
so many of them hiss
so many crude insults at her
that she gets up and leaves the room . . .
which gets them to start applauding—

When going to our lockers
means locker doors flung open just in time to hit us;

When entering a classroom
means isolation and whispers and cutting looks—

the walls of this school
are closing in.

DEMOCRACY

That vote, weeks ago,
Mr. Brittain, stay or go:
Who would win today?

MRS. ANDERSON

The meaner the hallways and classrooms get,
the kinder Mrs. Anderson gets,
the softer her eyes grow,
the closer her hugs draw me in,
the deeper her questions probe
about whether we feel safe and comfortable.
No matter what we say,
no matter how tightly we hold it in,
she knows the answer.

THANKSGIVING
(THURSDAY, NOVEMBER 22)

I am thankful for

my family of course

Gail Ann

Bobby and the other kids

the teachers at school,
especially Mrs. Anderson

our house
piano lessons
chicken divan
this turkey
my father's biscuits
my mother's chocolate pie
the sycamore tree

Grandmother Minnie,
who I'm already thankful for because she's family
but this is a special subset of thankful
for the clothes she makes me
(and that reminds me to be thankful for Sears
for having so many nice patterns
for Grandmother and me to choose from)

and another special subset of Grandmother-thankful
for the warm quilts that cover me
when I sleep at her farmhouse over in Oliver Springs,
for the farm's fresh
corn
blackberries
eggs

and the smell of coffee
Grandmother brews every morning,
which she pours into beautiful china cups
so we can breakfast like the ladies we are.

81

THEY'RE BACK
(MONDAY, NOVEMBER 26)

Over turkey and gravy
did they give thanks
and make plans to
give grief?

Over offered prayer,
did they beseech God
and prepare to
besmirch us?

"In Jesus's name,"
did they smear our names
and scheme to
smite us?

Who counts blessings,
only to crowd in the street
throwing rocks and screaming filth?
Who gives thanks,

only to gather in school
shoving and sneering and spitting?
Too many people for me to count.

They're on our route to school,
adults planted on the side of the road
just for the purpose of
spraying us with venom.

They're outside the school building,
adults and kids assembled
for the sport of hurling insults
and eggs.

They're inside the school building—
the Tennessee White Youth girls,
the boys whispering obscenities—
what has made them so bold?

This:
Just before Thanksgiving,
John Kasper was found not guilty
by an all-white jury of his peers
of charges that he incited the August riot.
When this verdict was announced,
the courtroom erupted in cheers.

Since then, going down the Hill
has been going downhill
for us;
and for them,
it's been Thanksgiving
every day.

82

ENOUGH
(TUESDAY, NOVEMBER 27)

Hands tearing our books.
Hands pulling our hair.
Mouths spewing insults.
(Do these mouths sing hymns on Sunday?
Do they say, "I love you"?)
The threats.
The scrawled, wicked notes.
Ink dumped into our lockers.
Target practice with nails and eggs—
and, oh, the pushing and shoving!
And those buttons,
KEEP WHITE SCHOOLS WHITE,
worn without any shame at all!
And the glint of knives,
shown off by some of the white boys.

It used to be that walking to school felt unsafe
and being inside school felt safe
enough.
No longer.

Outside school,
inside school,
our parents have discussed it,
we kids have discussed it, and it is
enough.
We will stay home.
We have to stay home.
Our school—
OUR SCHOOL!—
is against us.

> "NEGROES REMAIN HOME; INTIMIDATION
> INCREASES AT CLINTON HIGH SCHOOL
> Ugly language, egg throwing harass
> Negro students here"

—Clinton Courier-News, *November 29, 1956*

83

AN OFFER
(THURSDAY, NOVEMBER 29)

We've stayed at home
for three days now;
the school board has a huddle
where they discuss the goings-on
at Clinton High—the trouble,
the threatening, revolting taunts,
the violence against
us Negro students—in the face of law!
Are they incensed?

That's something I can't really know;
I only know that they
produce a plan they're offering
as something we should weigh.
The plan proposes that we leave—
go back to Austin High—
forget this integration thing. . . .
We gave it a nice try.
The board will help us work it out,

the details and the bus.
They think it might be best for all.

Consider it. Discuss.

84

WHAT ARE THEY THINKING?

We should quit?
Un-commit?
Simply split?

This wasn't fun and games.
No, we have aims.
And claims.

We claim: school is for blacks and whites.
We aim: to get our civil rights.
We aim: for peaceful days and nights.
We claim: school is for blacks and whites!

This plan is good if you're a fan
of the Klan.
It treats us as less than
every white man.
It can't stand.
We will finish what we began.

To be clear:
a bus to Knoxville again—
that's moving in the wrong
direction.

"We want to continue in Clinton High. That's where we belong."

—Jo Ann Allen, speaking to reporters

85

A VISIT
(MONDAY, DECEMBER 3)

When a white minister
calls your parents
to say he would like to escort
you and your friends
back to school,

and then the white minister
comes up the Hill
to plead with all of you
to return to Clinton High,

and you decide the white hate is still
too terrifying,

and then you think about what
this Reverend Paul Turner
of First Baptist Church said—

that it is your *moral right*;

well, when finally a white man agrees
desegregation is not just a matter of law and order,
but is a matter of *what is right,*

How do we not say *AMEN* to that?

We call Reverend Turner back.
Yes.
We will return.

"For we walk by faith, not by sight":
Second Corinthians, chapter 5, verse 7.
Yes.
We will walk.

86

THE SECOND BALLAD
OF THE HILL
(TUESDAY, DECEMBER 4)

Again we meet atop the Hill.
Again we share a prayer,
this time with Reverend Turner,
a man who seems to care.

He's white, this reverend, but he's here
to walk us down to school,
a way of showing how to live
the Bible's Golden Rule.

Off we go, the boys in front,
we girls a step behind.
The air is mild but we're chilled
by fears of what we'll find.

Will screaming crowds announce us,
or did the anger fade?
Softly, Reverend Turner says,

"Don't be afraid, don't be afraid."

At first, all quiet,
save some birds, our steps, and idle chatter.
At first—a cautious, easy stroll,
with nothing that's the matter.

But then we cross the railroad tracks,
and then we hear the crowd.
They're waiting in the street near school,
they're angry—and they're loud.

We see them then, the moms and dads,
with children by their side.
A wall of *NO*! A wall of *GO*!
Will we be denied?

"Don't be afraid, don't be afraid,"
Reverend Turner chants.
"Don't be afraid, don't be afraid"—
our watchwords through the rants.

They're throwing eggs, they're throwing rocks,
whizzing by our heads,
but we don't turn—we will not heed—
our eyes are straight ahead.

"Don't be afraid, don't be afraid."

We're almost at the door.

"Don't be afraid, don't be afraid."

We've made it through the war.

87

AND THEN

Did I even say good-bye
to Reverend Turner?
Did I thank him?
Did I thank the other two men
who walked with us
to show their support?
I don't know.
It's hard to think of niceties
like good-bye and thank you
when you're marching through a minefield.

We're in, he's out.
The reverend brings us
inside the front door
and we walk to our classes,
and he walks back down the steps,
and that is that,
except it isn't.

We are safe inside,
or as safe as we can feel inside anymore,

which is
not very,

but Reverend Turner is unsafe outside,
where a group of white people
jump him
beat him up
throw him against a plate-glass window
break that window
bang his head against the fender of a car
smash his nose

Are they going to *kill* him?

and when a white woman sees
and runs to the knot of people
surrounding Reverend Turner
runs to the knot to untie it
to help him,
another white woman,
part of the knot,
starts hitting and scratching *her.*

Will two people die today?

BREAKDOWN

We are safe inside until we aren't,
because a group of kids
who aren't even students here
break into school
scuffle with Mrs. Brittain
push her hard into the wall
yelling
"Let's get one of those niggers"
but they don't get anyone
a white student runs them off
they disappear

And then, before lunch:
Principal Brittain shuts the school down.

"We are going to close the school today, close
it tomorrow, and close it until it is safe for
children to attend."

—Principal David J. Brittain, statement to the public and press

NOTES TO MYSELF
IN THE SQUAD CAR

Was there no warning
this morning

that thugs would maul
Reverend Paul?

Could police have prevented
this demented

assault on a pastor,
avoided disaster,
gotten there faster?

You put me in this car to keep me secure—
Thanks.
But I'm not so sure
this is the cure

when bullies are allowed to roam the streets,
sticks, rocks, knives, spit—
sheets.

These people aren't all talk,
they don't just gawk,
these people stalk,

they draw blood.
Their stream of racism is a flood.

You take me home—
thanks—
while outlaws roam.

90

RESPONSIBLE
(TUESDAY NIGHT, DECEMBER 4)

Behind closed doors
at 437 Jarnigan Street,
Mom and I cry,
which makes Mamie cry,
which makes Herbie confused.
And it all makes my father
mad.

We are horrified:
If people will beat up
a man of God,
what *won't* they do?

We are fearful:
If boys will set upon
the home ec teacher,
who *won't* they strike?

We are—aren't we?—responsible:

If we had not set foot
in Clinton High School,
Reverend Turner wouldn't have called my mother,
wouldn't have walked us down the Hill today,
wouldn't have become the target of rage,
would be home peacefully tonight
working, I imagine,
on his next Sunday sermon.

And it all makes my father
mourn
    these people,
    our town;

and, yes, it makes him mad:
    Responsible?
    Don't look in this house.
    Don't look on this Hill.

REVEREND TURNER

A broken nose,
a swollen face.
He lives.
There is grace.

THE GOOD SAMARITAN

We don't know her name,
but like the unnamed
traveler in the Gospel of Luke
who stopped to help the half-dead man
on the winding road from Jerusalem to Jericho,

she did right.
Love your neighbor as yourself,
is the teaching.
The Good Samaritan learned it,
lived it,
and we hear she is fine.

SOME KIND OF VICTORY

We made that walk down the Hill
to claim the school for all of us.

We walked
again and again and again and again.

Did we win?
We walked to open doors.
Or did we lose?
Now those doors are shut.

I'll call it a bitter victory—
because if *we* can't be in school,
then school will be
for none of us.

NEXT TIME

Gail stayed home sick.
Or "sick"—
because her mother wouldn't let her
come to school.

So she missed it all,
and I have things to tell her

that come out
a jumble of
shuddering
shocking
panic.

Behind those cat-eye glasses,
there's that anger of hers,
which would have served her well
if she'd been there,
because anger pushes away
shuddering

shocking
panic.

In her dark eyes,
there's that doggedness of hers,
which comes from her aunt Mattie Bell,
which says she may have been "sick" this time,
but next time she'll be healthy
and stubborn and standing tall, because
if there's going to be a Clinton High School for anyone,
it will be for her.

95

BETTER LATE THAN NEVER
(WEDNESDAY, DECEMBER 5)

Judge Taylor,
who ordered the desegregation
of Clinton High School
exactly eleven months ago,
has had enough:
he's sending out federal marshals,
and they're armed with arrest warrants.
Those who turned yesterday into a
knock-down, drag-out
brawl—
the thugs, men and women,
who attacked Reverend Turner,
and the teenage boys
who broke into school
and roughed up Mrs. Brittain—
they are all to be arrested.
Sixteen warrants.
Sixteen names.
Bring them to jail, the judge says,

then to me
to be charged with this crime:
Contempt of a Court Order.

Contempt
has been floating around Clinton,
a noxious air
inhaled and exhaled
willfully,
reluctantly,
obliviously
(take your pick)
by the white people of this town—

and strangling us.

Finally, consequences.

96

ONE VOICE

The student council did it right away,
right after the school closed down.
Next the faculty council,
mayor,
newspaper editor,
and other white leaders followed.
They've written statements,
presented them to the school board,
all with the same requests:

Reopen Clinton High.
　Desegregate Clinton High.
　　Keep Principal Brittain in charge of Clinton High.
　　　Protect the students
　　　　of Clinton High.
　　　　　All of them.

They want to try again.
They want one school.

"I thought I didn't want the Negroes. Now I don't know. I wouldn't want to be like those people out there."

—*Unnamed white male student at Clinton High School, to Mrs. Margaret Anderson*

A REAL VICTORY
(THURSDAY, DECEMBER 6)

The day before yesterday,
the same day
we went down the Hill with Reverend Turner
and all that happened
happened,
there was also an election.
Not an election for president
(that was in November; Ike won again)
but for local officials
like the mayor and the city aldermen.

The results are in and

I don't know if people voted
after hearing what happened at school.
I don't know if people felt
things have gone too far.

I don't know if *A* led to *B* but—

every single
white supremacist
segregationist
candidate
lost.

Before all this,
before all that happened
happened,
I thought there was nothing I could do
about segregation.
I'm just a girl, I thought,
one girl who tries
to look at the good side of things,
because there's nothing I can do
about the bad.
I'm still that good-side-looking girl,
but now when I see the bad, I'll think—
I'll know—
there's something I can do about it.

"The tremendous defeat of the White Citizens Council's efforts to elect candidates in Tuesday's municipal election should end the political activity of that group and in addition should give notice to the law enforcement groups how the people of Clinton feel about maintaining law and order."

—*Editorial in the* Clinton Courier-News *written by editor Horace V. Wells Jr., December 6, 1956*

THEIR DECISION
(FRIDAY, DECEMBER 7)

The school board says
our school will reopen
on Monday,
December 10,
three days from today,

"barring any outbreaks of violence
over the week-end."

OUTBREAK

There's been a different sort of outbreak
here in my own house.
An outbreak of pessimism about what's possible
here in Clinton.
Not by me—
I'm an optimist!—
but by my father—
who's supposed to be an optimist.
These people, he says,
are just misled,
which I know is so much kinder
than what he could say.
But that's my pops—
These people are just misled.
Well, they've always been
misled,
so what's new?
What's new is
he's had enough.
Like us black students,

who had enough in November and stayed home.
Like Judge Taylor,
who had enough this week
and wrote out sixteen arrest warrants.
Like the people of Clinton,
who had enough and voted down the white supremacists.
But my dad can't stay home.
He can't arrest anyone.
He voted, but
he doesn't want to sit outside in the dark
with his hunting rifle
waiting for whoever might come in the dark.
(*These people.*)
He doesn't want to have to drive North
to find decent work.
(*These people.*)
He is not one to be beaten down,
so now he will rise up.
Which means the whole family must rise up with him.

100

"OUR" DECISION

We want to continue in Clinton High,
I told the newspapers.
That's where we belong.

We want.
We belong.
I want.
To belong.
It's our school.
I will finish what I started.

Jo Ann is stubborn.
Jo Ann is an optimist.
Jo Ann is not in charge.

My parents have made the decision:
We are leaving Clinton.
We are moving to California,
to Los Angeles, California.
My mother wants to stop worrying

every morning when I go to school.
My father wants to work in a good job.
My parents want their children to have better chances
than they think we will have in Clinton
or in Tennessee
or in all of the South.

I want
to finish what I started.
I want
to stick it out with my friends.
I want
to make Clinton High School
my school.
I want.
I belong.
It's our school.
But I am not going to get to finish what I started.

101

POPS SAYS THERE'S ALWAYS A BRIGHT SIDE

On the other hand

Palm trees, sunshine, Hollywood

It's California!

102

SEE US NOW

J. Robert Oppenheimer
Prime Minister Nehru of India
Polio
The Salk vaccine
Elections in Great Britain
Cigarettes and Cancer
The United Nations
Louis Armstrong
Grandma Moses
Egypt and Israel
Africa
The Suez Canal
Chou En-lai

are some of the important topics
covered by the most respected journalist
in television news,
Edward R. Murrow,
on his respected television show,
See It Now.

And next:
us.

Reporters and cameras
from *See It Now*
are all over Clinton,
to bring our story
to everyone, everywhere.
Dad and I are interviewed
right on our porch;
that'll be our nice house
people see on television.
My father talks about how
we are leaving
without hatred in our hearts.
I talk about how it felt
to face so much hatred.

The whole country
will see our faces
and hear our voices,
and I'm proud of that.

The whole country
will see Jo Ann Allen
walking away,

and that is a television show
I would rather switch off.

"They put signs on our lockers and told us to get out. And they threw paper at us. And they shoved us in the halls. And they threw chalk at us. And said all sorts of nasty things. And it just made me feel bad. And I couldn't concentrate at all on my lessons."

—*Jo Ann Allen, interviewed on* See It Now

"We're not leaving here with hatred in our hearts . . . because we realize that those people are just misled."

—*Herbert Allen, interviewed on* See It Now

PACKING UP

I'm packing up the clothes that my grandmother made;
I'm packing up the memories—I know they won't fade;
I'm packing up the pictures of our Easter parade;
I'm packing up my faith in the prayers we prayed;
I'm packing up my laughter at the games we played.

I'm packing up respect for the choices we weighed;
I'm packing up my pride in the progress we made;
I'm packing satisfaction in foundations we laid;
I'm packing up my doubts. . . .
    (What would happen if I stayed?
    Do my friends feel betrayed?)

I'm packing up my courage. I will not be afraid.

WORD CHOICES
(SUNDAY, DECEMBER 9)

Reverend Turner,
nose broken and swollen,
eye still black,
is preaching to his congregation.

"Here in Clinton, we are not especially against integration,"
he says.
"We are not especially against segregation.
But we are positively and definitely against the disintegration
of our community and our body politic."

Amen to that, I say, although I'm not there.
Negroes don't go to First Baptist.
I don't think we'd be welcome there,
Reverend Turner or no Reverend Turner.
And if we went, I'm sure
we couldn't walk in the front door.
But Reverend Turner's sermon is on everyone's lips.

I like that he said, *We are not especially against integration.*
I wish he didn't say, *We are not especially against segregation.*
That makes him sound like all the other white people
who would prefer we never went to Clinton High School,
who are only holding their noses
when we walk down the Hill and through the front door
because there's a court order,
and they want to be law-abiding people.

But maybe he felt he had to say
what he said
the way he said it
in front of the television cameras and
the hundreds of people crowded into his church,
some of whom felt sorry for him,
some proud,
some angry,
but most all of them positively not in favor of integration.

I like better what he said to reporters
who came to his house
the night after he was beaten:

> *I accompanied the Negro students to school*
> *to try to let my presence be testimony*
> *that as long as the law is what it is*
> *and as long as they have a desire to go to the school,*

it is their moral right to come unheckled and unhindered.

It is our moral right.
Unheckled and unhindered.
To go to school the same as any other kids,
no matter their skin color,
here
in Clinton, Tennessee,
there
in Los Angeles, California.

105

LEAVING BEHIND

Most furniture.
Most everything, really.
There isn't room in the car,
and shipping is expensive.

"White" and "colored" water fountains.
The buzzard's roost.
Libraries that aren't for me.
Restaurants that aren't for me.

The Hill.
The sycamore tree.
Honeysuckle.
Our nice house.
Mt. Sinai.
The life I've always known and,
except for these past months,
liked just fine.

Grandmother Minnie.

Aunt Mamie Lou.

My cousins.

Gail Ann.

Heart.

Ache.

106

GOOD-BYES

Even as I'm saying them,
these good-byes are a blur.
You'd think I'd want to fix them in my mind,
but maybe I would rather not.

These good-byes are a blur.
Neighbors and church friends to hug
(but maybe I would rather not)
and promises to make.

Neighbors and church friends to hug.
Maybe, maybe not, we will write.
And promises to make
maybe, maybe not, we will break.

Maybe, maybe not, we will write.
Not so for Gail and me.
Maybe, maybe not, we will break.
Not true for Gail and me.

Not so for Gail and me
the possibility of breaking bonds.
Not true for Gail and me
the possibility of losing touch.

The possibility of breaking bonds,
it would break me.
The possibility of losing touch,
that would leave me lost.

It would break me,
and so the blur protects; and words
that would leave me lost
leave my mind

even as I'm saying them.

107

DOWN THE HILL
(MONDAY, DECEMBER 10)

My father steers the Buick down the Hill,
the final time we drive (or walk) this way;
The streets are quiet, and the air is still;
We've said good-byes, and now we won't delay.
This morning, soon, my friends will yet again
approach the school we worked to make our own;
There won't be twelve of them, there won't be ten;
Just eight—I'm not the only one who's gone.
Here's Mamie by my side, and Herbie, too,
excited for the life that lies ahead;
I want to be excited, truly do,
but first must shed this feeling that I've fled.

Abandoning the cause that I embraced,
retreating from a stand I know is right.
The risks I took, the dangers that I faced—
what purpose served if I don't stay to fight?
What happened to my father's stubborn streak?
What happened to "You're good as anyone"?

Unchanged, he says, but here the future's bleak
when progress made becomes so soon undone.
What happened to my mother, straight and bold?
The one who speaks her mind, who doesn't wilt?
Those mobs, she says, so vile and uncontrolled
have threatened to destroy the life we've built.

I know. I know the fear my mother felt
to send me off to school into the fray.
To see me play the hand that we were dealt,
grim games with rules that change from day to day.
I felt it too, the dread, the hurt, the fear
of walking down our Hill to face the crowd.
But also felt the thrill, the pride, the cheer
of showing all that we would not be cowed.
Our town, our school, our lives are changed for good.
We crossed a line, we twelve, and reached a goal.
Knocked down, pushed back, abused, yet still we stood
as proof that, joined together, we are whole.

And as the miles move beneath the wheels
I smile; the optimist inside me heals.

108

FOR THE RECORD

"We're leaving for California today . . . because I want my kids to have a better break than I did.

I don't believe there will be an opportunity for my children in Tennessee because no matter how much education they get here, there's no place for them to use it.

I guess you'd call me stubborn for letting the school situation keep me in Clinton this long, but now that integration seems assured I want to go where my children will have a chance.

You see, I had a chance for a job in California last summer but we didn't go. Jo Ann and I are both stubborn and we thought we'd just tough it out.

Someday, a long time in the future, she's going to be a doctor—a pediatrician.

I think everything will be all right in Clinton now that the FBI has stepped in, but you never know.

Sometimes you have a big fire and a rain comes along and puts it out and you hope it's all over. But then when it's dry, a little smoke comes out, and then more smoke, and finally a wind comes along and whoosh, up goes the blaze again. Well, this is the rainy time, but there's still a little smoke around. . . .

In fact, a lot of white people have been mighty sympathetic with our cause. But I can't take it any more. We're going to California."

—Herbert Allen, "Here's Why Jo Ann Allen
Didn't Go To Clinton High This Morning,"
Chicago Defender, *December 10, 1956*

"The kids could work things out for themselves. If grownups would teach them love instead of hate, we'd get along just wonderfully."

—Jo Ann Allen, *interviewed after arriving in California,* Los Angeles Sentinel, *December 20, 1956*

"After going to all-Negro schools for 10 years, and a practically all-caucasian school for four months, Dorsey [High] is new and different. Going to a school in an atmosphere of friendliness toward all is a wonderful experience."

—Jo Ann Allen, *on how she likes her new high school in Los Angeles,* Los Angeles Sentinel, *March 28, 1957*

EPILOGUE

A s Jo Ann and her family drove out of Clinton on Monday, December 10, 1956, the students of Clinton High School returned to classes without violence or incident. Principal Brittain convened a school-wide assembly in which the Anderson County Attorney read a court order to the somber students. "It is not my intention to tell you what to think," he said. "Nor is it my desire to tell you what to believe. But it is my duty to tell you how to act in the future, so long as you are students at Clinton High School." Among the behaviors that the official warned would no longer be tolerated: throwing things, messing up lockers, crude language, pushing and shoving, and sending threatening notes to teachers.

But the true acceptance that Jo Ann hoped for from her white classmates did not come about. Neither did friendships between the black and white students. At best, the white students tolerated the black students who remained. At worst, they continued to engage in harassing, if not violent, behaviors.

Only six of the original twelve African American students who enrolled in August 1956 were still in Clinton High School at the end of the 1956–1957 school year. Bobby Cain was one of them. He graduated Clinton High School on May 17, 1957—three years to the day after the Supreme Court handed down the *Brown v. Board* decision. Bobby's graduation marked the first time an African American student graduated from an integrated state high school in Tennessee.

David J. Brittain resigned as Clinton High School's principal soon after graduation. As he said in a television interview, "I can frankly say that I've suffered nothing but personal harassment, and other people [have] too. . . . It just presses you down every day lower and lower."

Later in the summer of 1957, sixteen people, including John Kasper, were brought to trial for the violence of December 4, 1956. Kasper received a six-month jail sentence. Others received lesser sentences.

Gail Ann Epps stuck it out at Clinton High School for the 1957–1958 school year, her senior year. With Jo Ann gone, Gail Ann was the only black student in her class. She graduated in May 1958, becoming the first female African American student to graduate from an integrated state high school in Tennessee.

None of the other Clinton 12 graduated from Clinton High School. Some left town to attend school under less stressful conditions. Some dropped out and never finished high school.

The remaining black students—and the new ones who enrolled—continued to face racist animosity. This animosity blew up—quite literally—on Sunday morning, October 5, 1958, when a dynamite explosion destroyed the school. Fortunately, the school was empty at the time of the explosion. No one was injured. The identity of those who dynamited the school has never been uncovered.

If anti-integration malcontents and white supremacists thought they could blow up desegregation in Clinton, they were wrong. Students—black and white—were bused to an empty elementary school building in Oak Ridge, about fifteen miles away. If anything, the bombing pulled the community together around the high school. It attracted even more attention from the nation at large. People across the country donated funds to help rebuild Clinton High School. A famous newspaper columnist, Drew Pearson, spearheaded a national campaign calling on high school students everywhere to give the price of one bottle of Coca-Cola. The money poured in. Renowned evangelist Reverend Billy Graham came to Clinton, preaching to a packed audience on the need for racial peace, and supporting fundraising efforts for rebuilding. When Clinton High School reopened in the fall of 1960, black and white students continued to attend. The school never went back to segregation.

It wasn't until 1965 that black children were admitted to the all-white elementary school in Clinton and the all-black Green McAdoo Grammar School closed. In August 2006, the former school for black children reopened as the Green McAdoo Cultural Center, a museum commemorating the Clinton 12, with exhibits that tell the story of the desegregation of Clinton High School. Congressman John Lewis of Georgia, a famous leader of the civil rights movement, spoke at the dedication of the museum. He said that when he heard about the events in Clinton as a young man, the news inspired him to take a stand against racial injustice. To the people assembled for the Green McAdoo dedication—black people, white people, people who had participated in the events of 1956, and people who had not—Congressman Lewis said, "We are one people. We all live in the same house."

MORE ABOUT JO ANN

Immediately upon arriving in Los Angeles in December 1956, Jo Ann and her family were sought out by news reporters wanting to hear about their experiences. "Let me tell you the good things first," Jo Ann said to a reporter from the *Baltimore Afro-American*, for an article published on January 5, 1957. The article, headlined "Jo Ann Allen, heroine of Clinton school fight, interviewed at new Calif. home," continued:

" 'There were a lot of good things,' Jo Ann said quickly. 'I was elected vice president of my [home]room last August. Then there was the plane trip to Washington. I went along with a white girl and her mother.' "

Then Jo Ann detailed the "other things" for the newspaper reporter—the violence and bullying and nastiness—and concluded with the story of Reverend Turner's heroism, which she said showed that "not everybody is against integration." The article concluded, "But Miss Allen is glad that she is here."

Jo Ann settled into her new life. She attended an integrated high school in Los Angeles. She continued to be in demand as a speaker—though she was still only fifteen—at events where people wanted to hear about Clinton. The CBS television network broadcast Edward R. Murrow's *See It Now* episode, titled "Clinton and the Law," on Sunday, January 6, 1957. This brought even greater attention to the twelve students who had succeeded— at great personal risk—in desegregating a white Southern high school. In Los Angeles, Jo Ann appeared onstage with baseball legend Jackie Robinson, where they were both hailed as heroes of the civil rights movement.

In 1958, Jo Ann graduated from Dorsey High School in Los Angeles and pursued the dream she had told her homeroom about back in August of 1956—the dream of becoming a nurse. She completed nursing school in 1963 and went on to have a career as a pediatric nurse—that is, a nurse specializing in the care of babies and children—for forty years. Jo Ann also continued singing, performing R & B and jazz in venues around Los Angeles. With her husband, Victor E. Boyce, Jo Ann is the proud mother of two sons and a daughter, and has four grandchildren.

And, although they live across the country from each other, Jo Ann and Gail Ann (who stayed in Tennessee) still call each other best friends.

CLINTON IN CONTEXT

In 1956, accounts of the events surrounding the desegregation of Clinton High School were splashed across the front pages of newspapers and magazines throughout the United States. The stories came into living rooms on the nightly television news.

Eyes across America were on the little town, and on Jo Ann and her classmates, as Clinton High School became the first desegregated state high school in Tennessee and, by most accounts, the first in the South. A year after the events described in this book, *Time* magazine observed, "Of all the integration hotspots of 1956, Clinton, Tenn., was the hottest." Four years on, the events remained uppermost in the mind of Margaret Anderson, the teacher who offered so much support and empathy to Jo Ann and other members of the Clinton 12. In a cover story for the *New York Times Magazine,* Mrs. Anderson wrote of "mob violence in the town and an almost complete state of insurrection within the school." She noted: "I would not want any community to undergo the racial troubles of Clinton."

And yet today, relatively few people know about what happened in Clinton, Tennessee. These events, so consequential in civil rights history and so widely known in their day, became lost to most Americans. A year later, a vicious new desegregation crisis took place at Central High School in Little Rock, Arkansas. Three years after that, a desegregation drama in New Orleans caught the nation's attention. These two later events, not the crisis in Clinton, have become the iconic symbols of the struggle for school desegregation.

In the Little Rock crisis, in September 1957, the governor of Arkansas himself, Orval Faubus, refused to obey court orders to desegregate the schools. In contrast to Clinton—where Governor Frank Clement sent in the National Guard to uphold the African American students' right to go to Clinton High

School—Governor Faubus sent in soldiers to *prevent* black students from attending Central High. Faubus sided with white segregationists, who took to the streets violently to resist desegregation. President Dwight D. Eisenhower finally dispatched the 101st Airborne Division of the U.S. Army to Little Rock to protect the "Little Rock 9," as the African American students became known, in their bid to enter Central High School. Not to be outdone, Governor Faubus then closed down the public schools rather than proceed with integration.

In New Orleans, a court order to desegregate the elementary schools sent six-year-old Ruby Bridges to the all-white William Frantz Elementary School in November 1960. Because of threats of violence from white segregationists, United States marshals accompanied Ruby on her walk to school every day of the 1960–1961 school year. Many white parents took their children out of the school permanently rather than send their children to a school attended by a single black student. And inside the school, only one teacher agreed to teach Ruby. Ruby Bridges became the single child in that teacher's class; she was a first-grade class of one. Despite her isolation, and the pressure on her and her parents to quit, she never missed a day of school that year. Ruby's persistence and bravery became headlines across the country.

Meanwhile, Clinton faded from the collective American memory. Why?

Perhaps it's because the Clinton story has more shades of gray than others. That is, while the Clinton crisis definitely featured ardent white segregationists and white supremacists, it also included white local leaders who, however reluctantly, decided to follow the law after *Brown v. Board of Education*. While the Clinton crisis featured violence against black students, it also included violence against white leaders who aligned themselves with desegregation. And while Clinton High School bumped along toward desegregation, never to turn back to segregation despite all obstacles, Little Rock featured the dramatic shutdown of the public schools by the Arkansas governor— and New Orleans isolated a little black girl in a classroom by herself, which is surely not the definition of "desegregation."

Perhaps, also, imagery seared Little Rock and New Orleans into the public consciousness. The hatred faced by the Little Rock 9 was dramatically captured by a newspaper photographer on September 4, 1957. In his photo, Elizabeth Eckford, one of the black students, is shown as she is cruelly taunted by a white teenage girl. The picture was transmitted around the world and remains a recognizable and iconic image to this day. And the desegregation of William Frantz Elementary School in New Orleans was presented to the world by Norman Rockwell, a famous artist, who created a painting of Ruby Bridges walking to school, flanked by U.S. marshals. The painting was entitled, *The Problem We All Live With*. Millions of people saw the image when it was published on the cover of *Look* magazine.

"Firsts" are a tricky business. We like to be able to point to an accomplishment that was the "first" of its kind. Those who have studied and documented the Clinton 12 say that those students were the first to integrate a state high school in the South after *Brown*. (You can find this assertion in the *Tennessee Encyclopedia of History and Culture*, in a Library of Congress exhibit commemorating *Brown v. Board*, in books, scholarly papers, and countless news articles.) The Clinton 12 heard this as they went through their ordeal, and afterward. And yet—further digging reveals that the tiny town of Charleston, Arkansas, desegregated its high school on August 23, 1954, two years before Clinton and three years before Little Rock. How has this milestone escaped notice? Perhaps because of this: the town leaders kept the desegregation plans secret in an effort to limit public (white) backlash. There are no dramatic photos from the Charleston, Arkansas, events. There are no front-page *New York Times* stories.

First, last, or somewhere in the middle, all the African American students who braved their way into schools where they knew they were not wanted inspire admiration and awe.

THE OTHER MEMBERS OF THE CLINTON 12

ALFRED WILLIAMS was a senior during the 1956–1957 school year, but he did not graduate. He was expelled from Clinton High School in the spring of 1957, after he got in a fight with white students who were threatening Maurice Soles, who was Alfred's younger brother. Because of this expulsion, Alfred never graduated from high school. "I want to tell you we were nervous," Alfred told the *Washington Post* in 2006, on the fiftieth anniversary of the Clinton crisis. "When this school integrated, you could see the hate in people." Alfred worked for many years on the maintenance staff at Clinton Elementary School, where he shared with young students the lessons of his experience desegregating Clinton High School.

ALVAH JAY LAMBERT (MCSWAIN) was the fifteenth child in a family of nineteen children. Her family name is forever linked to the Clinton desegregation crisis in law books, in the case of *McSwain v. County Board of Education*. That was the lawsuit brought on behalf of Alvah's older sister Joheather, and others, in 1950—four years before *Brown v. Board of Education*—challenging the segregated system of high school education in Clinton. Judge Robert L. Taylor ruled against them in 1952, but he then reversed his ruling after the 1954 U.S. Supreme Court decision in *Brown v. Board*. It was too late for Joheather, who was done with high school by then, so it was Alvah, a freshman, and the other Clinton 12 students who became the desegregation pioneers in Clinton in the fall of 1956. Despite all the efforts the McSwains put into desegregating Clinton High School, the family moved to Los Angeles, California, in May 1957. Once there, Alvah had to quit high school after tenth grade to help care for her ill grandmother. She returned to school four years later, along with her mother, Winona McSwain, and mother and daughter graduated from John C. Fremont High School together. "That was one of the happiest days of my life," Alvah wrote in an essay for the Green McAdoo Cultural Center website.

Alvah, who enjoyed being outdoors, worked as a truck driver for many years.

ANNA THERESSER CASWELL completed her freshman, sophomore, and junior years at Clinton High School. She then decided to withdraw from Clinton and attend night school at Austin High School. In an interview in 2017, Anna Theresser said of that first year of desegregation, "It was lonely. We weren't allowed to do any of the fun stuff that they were doing at school." In an earlier interview with a reporter for a church newspaper, she said, "I was jumpy all the time. . . . I never saw any of the other black kids. There were two white people who would talk to me. Can you imagine going to school all day and only talking to two people?" Anna Theresser worked for many years at Martin Marietta Energy Systems in Oak Ridge, Tennessee, and has been a foster mother to many children.

BOBBY CAIN, a senior when he walked down the Hill to enter Clinton High School for the first time in August 1956, graduated from the school on May 17, 1957, as the first African American male to graduate from an integrated state high school in Tennessee. He went on to Tennessee State University, and worked at the National Laboratory in Oak Ridge, Tennessee, after receiving his college degree. Bobby served in the army during the Vietnam War, worked at Vanderbilt University after his military service, and later worked in state government in Nashville, Tennessee. In the worst of the fray that accompanied the Clinton High School desegregation, Bobby came close to just leaving school, he told a newspaper reporter years later. "I was wondering if it was worth it. But I knew I had to think of my brothers and sisters. It was not just for me."

GAIL ANN UPTON (EPPS) completed her junior and senior years at Clinton High School, graduating in May of 1958. She was the first African American female to graduate from an integrated state high school in Tennessee. She then attended Tennessee State University and worked as a substitute teacher at Green McAdoo School. "I lived in a predominantly white neighborhood. I played with little white kids," Gail described her childhood in Clinton in a 2017 interview. "It was comfortable. My grandmother fed many a white kid." But the school desegregation crisis showed her another side of race relations: "I never realized that people would be that mean. . . . My mother said she noticed a difference in me. From then on, when a white person would say something, I would go off. But through prayer I got through it." In an essay she wrote for the Green McAdoo Cultural Center website, Gail Ann reflected, "The Clinton desegregation has made an impact on my life. . . . Also it makes me proud to have helped make it easier for other generations to come after me."

MAURICE SOLES, younger brother of Alfred Williams, was a freshman at Clinton High School from 1956 to 1957. He did not complete high school. After working in the Clinton area, he served in the U.S. Army in the Vietnam War, where he was seriously wounded. Maurice moved to Phoenix, Arizona; received his GED (high school equivalency) there; and eventually moved back to Clinton and worked in business with another of his brothers. He died in 2011.

MINNIE ANN JONES (DICKEY) and her family moved to Knoxville at the end of the 1956–1957 school year. In remarks she provided to the Green McAdoo Cultural Center website, Minnie Ann wrote, thinking back on her experience at Clinton High School, "I really did not know that people could be so mean and hateful. I guess you could say that I took away a sense of pride. . . ." Asked what advice she would give young people today, she added that they should "Make the most of whatever you have and not to put someone else down for having less than you do, but to help that person if you can." Minnie Ann worked in various positions in Knoxville, and also served as a foster grandparent.

REGINA SMITH (TURNER) attended Clinton High School for two years, her sophomore and junior years. For her senior year, she went to Tallahassee, Florida, to live with an aunt and finish high school there in a segregated school. Years later, she explained to an interviewer, "In Clinton it was just go to school and come home. We couldn't go to football or basketball games or any social event at school. I wanted more than that." She added: "I was too angry to be afraid. I hope I never get so angry again." Regina returned to Tennessee after high school. She attended Knoxville Business College and had a long career at Modine Manufacturing Company.

ROBERT THACKER, a junior in 1956–1957, left Clinton High School during that school year. He moved to Mount Clemens, Michigan, where he graduated from high school in 1958 and then enlisted in the U.S. Army. Robert went on to work for Ford Motor Company. He then founded his own trucking company in Pontiac, Michigan.

RONALD GORDON "POOCHIE" HAYDEN started his freshman year at Clinton High School in the fall of 1956. He was known as a serious and quiet student, with dreams of becoming a lawyer. However, Poochie became gravely ill during the 1956–1957 school year. Diagnosed with a brain tumor, he had to withdraw from Clinton High School. Poochie underwent several surgeries, which left him legally blind. However, he went on to continue his education at the School for the Blind in Talladega, Alabama. He died in 1966 at the age of twenty-three.

WILLIAM LATHAM left Clinton High School after the school was bombed in October 1958. He later received his GED, served in the U.S. Army, and worked as a driver in New Jersey. Upon his retirement, he returned to Tennessee to live in Oak Ridge.

WRITING THIS BOOK

A Note from Jo Ann: "You should write a book, Ms. Boyce." It's a remark I've heard frequently over the past twenty-five years when presenting the Clinton 12 story to young scholars.

Well, it's always been a dream of mine, yet no matter how many attempts I made, no matter how copious the notes I wrote, I could never quite succeed at putting this story to paper for a book—until now. More than sixty years after taking those steps down the Hill on August 27, 1956, I finally get to put my experiences in a book about a pivotal point in the history of the United States. It is just my blessing to have the help of Debbie Levy as my coauthor. (She doesn't want me to remind you that she's a noted award-winning author of books for young people, but I am doing it anyway!) It doesn't get any better than that for me.

It has long been my contention that hatred is a disease of the heart. This is not a disease a person is born with; instead, it is one that is taught. It is brought about through those who teach it to their children. They learned it from their parents and grandparents, who learned it from their parents and grandparents, and on and on. It has gone on for generations. How absurd and insidious to infect one's children with this vicious disease! How vicious to teach them to inflict it on others—for example, to inflict it on me and the other Clinton 12 members. Hatred leaves holes in the heart, a scarred mind, and a wasted brain—and I am speaking of its effects on those who hold this disease in their hearts and inflict it on others.

When I was growing up in Clinton, my white neighbors and I got along perfectly fine. We played together, ate from one another's tables, and shared food when the need arose. So what, pray tell, would cause those neighbors to turn against us during the desegregation of Clinton High School? I believe it was probably long-held beliefs of white superiority over people of color, beliefs passed on to them by their ancestors, beliefs that went underground, perhaps, while we played and ate and shared—but that never really went away. I'd add the emotion of fear to the mix too—fear of the possibility that we would learn as much as, or more than, they; fear that we might get better jobs, have more opportunities, gain more power. Of course, our intent in desegregating was simply to continue our education in our own hometown, our own school system, our own backyard, where it was rightfully ours to do. We weren't doing something *against* anybody; we were doing something to better our lives and, presumably, to improve our community.

I don't get hate. I never have and never will. It is an unnecessary, tiring, narrow-minded, deeply disturbing way to view our fellow humans. Why do people denigrate those of other ethnicities, races, religious beliefs, and gender identities? Why reject others who look different from our own group? I just mentioned fear and long-held prejudices passed down over generations, but I wish I had a more complete answer. However, this question has led me and inspired me, year after year, to tell this story and encourage the young people of the United States to be torchbearers, to take up the baton and run the race—to help rid ourselves of a heart disease that need not exist at all.

Among the greatest rewards I've reaped from sharing the Clinton 12 story over these past decades are letters from students who have heard my presentation when I visited their schools. To me, these hundreds of letters are treasures. Of course I appreciate their expressions of thanks for what the Clinton 12 did. Even more, I appreciate their recognition of the continuing need for change in how we human beings treat one another. There have been the young scholars who, contemplating the hatred that erupted in Clinton, Tennessee, wrote, "Thank you for teaching us about the difference between hate and anger," and "I have learned that when someone hates you, don't hate them back." There have been the students who, considering the ways the Clinton 12 dealt with adversity, let me know that, "The thing that impacted me most was the fact you chose to see life positively," and "I am very impressed at your ability to resist the urge to strike back violently." And there have been the students who understand that when we stand up for what is right, we're not only standing up for ourselves, but also for others whom we don't even know—and for the future: "Your courage to walk to that school—I bet it encouraged other people to not be afraid." "You and the rest of the Clinton 12 did a great thing for blacks, immigrants, and the world." "The Clinton 12 helped change history."

Let's keep changing history.

One more thing, on the use of a certain word in this book. I heard this word constantly during the worst times at Clinton High School, although it's presented only three times in the pages you've just read. It was poison spewed at me and my black friends by white racists, adults and children. It's one of the most vile words in the language. It is profoundly dehumanizing, hurtful, and offensive. I don't want to give this word airtime— but I also want readers to understand how disturbing it felt to hear that word. I don't believe its impact on me and my friends is conveyed by rendering it as "n——." We did not hear anyone say "n, dash-dash-dash-dash-dash." We heard a word that cut like a knife—a filthy knife.

A Note from Debbie: I wish I could have known Jo Ann when she was fifteen. I first got a glimpse of who she was when, on YouTube, I found the *See It Now* CBS television news show that aired in January 1957 about the crisis in Clinton. There she is on the screen, speaking with both frustration and patience about the struggle of being one of twelve black students at Clinton High School. This was one poised teenager.

I got additional glimpses of the teenage Jo Ann when I read newspaper interviews she gave during and after the Clinton crisis. Her comments to the *Baltimore Afro-American* newspaper in January 1957 were typical. The reporter asked Jo Ann to describe her experience in Clinton. "Let me tell you the good things first," she responded. Here, I thought, is a person with a heart as big as the movement she advanced. No wonder the headline of that story read "Jo Ann Allen, heroine of Clinton school fight."

Jo Ann and I connected in the spring of 2015, after her daughter-in-law, Libby Boyce, put a post about her and the Clinton 12 on Facebook, and my literary agent, Caryn Wiseman, brought it to my attention. We hit it off, and then proceeded to work for more than two years to produce a manuscript draft, going back and forth with telephone calls and long emails (we live across the country from each other); visiting Clinton, Tennessee, together; and working through the shape and scope of this book. So much here is pure Jo Ann, straight out of our interviews, conversations, and her writings.

As for writing this book of nonfiction in verse, the format practically chose itself. When I listened to fifteen-year-old Jo Ann talking on camera in the old *See It Now* show, I was struck by the musicality of her voice. As I came to know the adult Jo Ann during our collaboration, I continued to delight in her musical voice and wasn't surprised to learn that she sang professionally and loves poetry. A book in verse seemed a natural fit for Jo Ann's voice, but there was more to it: we found that the emotional and often urgent cadences that poetry delivers were qualities that fit the story we set out to tell, not only the person at the center of the telling. The book is mostly written in free verse, but many chapters are presented in more structured forms of metrical and rhyming verse (sonnet, ballad, villanelle, pantoum, haiku, and other patterns). These, too, were intended to illuminate the story and to honor Jo Ann's voice which—as readers know by now!—has always reflected her mother's insistence on "the King's English."

The story of the Clinton 12 is the story of doing something hard to help people who will follow in your footsteps. It's about doing something that is deeply uncomfortable to you but that you know is right. It's about the choice between being a follower and being a leader. And it's about maintaining dignity and pride under duress.

Today, Jo Ann will be the first to remind you that she is just one of twelve black students who went through the agonizing experience of desegregating Clinton High School. She'll make sure you know that because of her parents' decision to leave, she spent only one semester there. The heroes, she'll say, are Bobby Cain and Gail Ann Epps—the ones who hung in there long enough to graduate despite the danger and discomfort of showing up, day after day, to a place where they knew they were not wanted.

I say they are all heroes.

Poetic Forms: Among the poetic forms used in this book are **Acrostic** (40, "Do the Math"); **Ballad** (23, "The Ballad of the Hill," 37, "Peacekeepers," and 86, "The Second Ballad of the Hill"); **Cascade** (67, "Incidents"); **Cinquain** (5, III, "Last Year: Vine Junior High," and 5, IV, "This Year: Austin High School"); **Haiku** (64, "And Then There Are the Thumbtacks," 78, "Democracy," and 101, "Pops Says There's Always a Bright Side"); **Ode** (4, "Keep Your Head Up," and 32, "You Are as Good"); **Pantoum** (106, "Good-Byes"); **Sonnet** (42, "This Time," and 107, "Down the Hill"); and **Villanelle** (22, "The Night Before"). In addition, rhyming poems with various stanza forms (such as couplets and quatrains) and rhyming patterns make up the poems in 5, I, "The Green McAdoo Grammar School"; 8, "Me, Myself, and I"; 28, "Storm Brewing"; 39, "First Monday of September"; 48, "Gone"; 57, "Boom"; 60, "Who Did It"; 83, "An Offer"; 84, "What Are They Thinking?"; 89, "Notes to Myself in the Squad Car"; 91, "Reverend Turner"; and 103, "Packing Up."

A FINAL NOTE

In 1956, the white leadership of Clinton, Tennessee—the mayor, the school board, the city council, law enforcement officials, the school principal, religious leaders, many in the business and legal community—acknowledged that the Supreme Court's ruling in *Brown v. Board of Education* meant that Clinton High School could no longer remain segregated. As they said and wrote repeatedly, they implemented desegregation because it was the "law of the land" and they believed in "law and order."

But: if a court order had not required the school to integrate, these people would have continued to support segregation. They did not embrace racial equality as a human right.

These stinting, ungenerous attitudes made the experiences of the African American students who pioneered integration at Clinton High School more bitter and isolating than they had to be. Reverend Paul Turner finally realized just how wrong the attitudes of his fellow white citizens were when he risked his life to walk the students down the Hill. But Turner had few white allies who embraced this view.

What happened in Clinton illuminates Dr. Martin Luther King Jr.'s observation seven years later when he wrote:

"I have almost reached the regrettable conclusion that the Negro's great stumbling block in the stride toward freedom is not the White Citizens Councillor or the Ku Klux Klanner but the white moderate who is more devoted to order than to justice. . . . Lukewarm acceptance is much more bewildering than outright rejection."

True acceptance—not stingy tolerance, not begrudging endurance—is the way toward justice.

SCRAPBOOK

A sign at the city limits of Clinton, Tennessee, in 1956.

Walking down the Hill toward Clinton High School, left to right: Bobby Cain, Robert Thacker, Maurice Soles, Gail Ann Epps, Alvah McSwain (behind Gail Ann), Jo Ann Allen, Ronald Hayden, Alfred Williams, Regina Turner, and Minnie Ann Dickey.

White students picketing on the first day of desegregation of Clinton High School.

Jo Ann and Bobby walking home after school.

Crowds of white people gathering outside Clinton High School.

Gathered in a hallway inside school, left to right: Maurice Soles, Ronald Hayden, Robert Thacker, Alvah McSwain, and Anna Theresser Caswell.

Jo Ann in a classroom in Clinton High, isolated from the white students.

Thousands of whites outside the courthouse protesting the desegregation of Clinton High School.

White mob terrorizing African Americans who traveled through Clinton during Labor Day weekend.

National Guard vehicles in the streets of Clinton after the Labor Day weekend riots.

National Guardsmen protecting U.S. Navy seaman James Grant Chandler, who had been visiting Gail Ann Epps, after a white mob threatened him as he walked to the bus station.

National Guardsmen and white people arrested in connection with violence during desegregation protests.

Jo Ann and Minnie Ann Dickey exiting Clinton High School.

Reverend Paul Turner (center, black hat and coat), with three of the students he escorted down the Hill to return to school on December 4, 1956; from left to right, students are Minnie Ann Dickey, Jo Ann, and Alvah McSwain.

Jo Ann as a senior at Dorsey High School, Los Angeles, California.

Clinton High School rubble after the bombing on October 5, 1958.

Jo Ann Allen Boyce visiting
Clinton, Tennessee, in 2017.

Jo Ann Allen Boyce and
Gail Ann Upton in 2017.

TIMELINE OF SCHOOL DESEGREGATION AND CIVIL RIGHTS LANDMARKS

U.S. school desegregation milestones are in this type.

Clinton milestones are in this type.

Other U.S. civil rights milestones are in this type.

July 1868 The Fourteenth Amendment to the U.S. Constitution is ratified. It says, among other things, that no state may "deny to any person within its jurisdiction the equal protection of the laws."

....

May 1896 In the case of *Plessy v. Ferguson*, the U.S. Supreme Court rules that racial segregation by a state does not violate the Fourteenth Amendment if "separate but equal" facilities or accommodations are provided for African Americans. *Plessy* involves segregation on trains—Homer Plessy, a black man, was arrested for choosing to travel in a whites-only railway car in violation of a Louisiana law. One Supreme Court justice, John Harlan, dissents from the ruling. "Our Constitution is color-blind," he writes, "and neither knows nor tolerates classes among citizens. In respect of civil rights, all citizens are equal before the law." The *Plessy* decision's separate-but-equal rule comes to apply to all manner of segregation, including in schools.

....

November 1908 The U.S. Supreme Court, in the case of *Berea College v. Kentucky*, rules that Kentucky may require a private college to operate as a whites-only, segregated school despite the wishes of the college to admit black students.

....

November 1927 In *Gong Lum v. Rice*, the Supreme Court rules that Mississippi may define a student of Chinese ancestry as "colored" for purposes of the state constitution, which provides that "Separate schools shall be maintained for children of the white and colored races," and that excluding the student from all-white schools does not violate her rights under the U.S. Constitution's Equal Protection Clause.

....

December 1938 The Supreme Court orders Missouri's all-white law school to admit a black student in the case of *Missouri ex rel. Gaines v. Canada*. The Court is not overturning the separate-but-equal rule, but states that the black student must be enrolled because Missouri has no separate law school for African Americans.

....

June 1950 In *Sweatt v. Painter*, the Supreme Court rules that excluding African Americans from Texas's whites-only law school, and offering them instead admission to a new, blacks-only law school, violates the Fourteenth Amendment to the Constitution. While not rejecting *Plessy v. Ferguson* outright, the Court finds that isolating black students in their own law school does not provide a legal education equal to that of the education available in the whites-only law school.

....

December 1950 Parents of black high-school-aged students in Clinton seek their children's admittance to all-white Clinton High School, arguing that they should not be required to attend a distant all-black high school. School and government officials refuse, and the parents file a lawsuit in federal district court. The case is called *McSwain v.*

County Board of Education of Anderson County. The families involved in the lawsuit include the McSwains and the Dickeys, whose younger children will eventually become part of the Clinton 12. Among the lawyers representing Clinton's black families in this case: Thurgood Marshall. Four years later, Marshall and other lawyers will convince the U.S. Supreme Court that school segregation is unconstitutional (see below, "May 1954") in the groundbreaking *Brown v. Board of Education* case. In 1967, Marshall will become the first African American appointed to the Supreme Court.

....

April 1951 Barbara Johns, a junior at the all-black Robert R. Moton High School in Farmville, Virginia, in Prince Edward County, organizes a strike to protest the abysmal conditions at the underfunded, overcrowded segregated school. The strike leads to a lawsuit challenging segregation, which later becomes one of the cases the Supreme Court considers when it decides *Brown v. Board of Education.*

....

April 1952 In *McSwain v. County Board of Education of Anderson County,* Judge Robert L. Taylor rules that Clinton High School need not open its doors to African American students, and that their constitutional rights are not violated by being barred from the local all-white school in Clinton.

....

May 1954 In *Brown v. Board of Education,* the Supreme Court rules that separate schools for black and white children are "inherently unequal" and deprive black children of the equal protection of law guaranteed by the Fourteenth Amendment. The unanimous ruling overturns *Plessy* as applied to public education. The Supreme Court puts off for a future date the questions of exactly when and how the decree should be carried out.

....

May 1955 In *Brown v. Board of Education II*, the Supreme Court rules on the issue of implementing its decision of the previous year. The Court states that school authorities must make a "prompt and reasonable start" toward admitting black children to white schools, but it also allows that, "Once such a start has been made, the courts may find that additional time is necessary to carry out the ruling in an effective manner." In any event, the Court rules that school desegregation must proceed "with all deliberate speed."

....

August 1955 In northwest Mississippi, two white men kidnap and brutally murder Emmett Till, a black teenager visiting from Chicago, Illinois. The white men were offended because Till allegedly whistled at a white woman. Till's murder arouses outrage around the country. At his funeral, his mother insists that her son's casket remain open for viewing, so that the nation and world can see the violence that was committed against him. An all-white jury acquits the two killers of all criminal charges.

....

December 1955 Rosa Parks, an African American woman, refuses to give up her seat on the bus in Montgomery, Alabama, to a white person, as the law requires. She is arrested for breaking Montgomery's segregation law. Her arrest prompts black citizens, led by Dr. Martin Luther King Jr., to organize the Montgomery Bus Boycott in protest. Although most of the bus system's customers are African Americans, bus operators refuse to discontinue their segregationist practices.

....

January 1956 Judge Robert L. Taylor of the federal district court in Tennessee reconsiders the case of *McSwain v. County Board of Education of Anderson County* and this time rules that the all-white

Clinton High must admit black students "not later than the beginning of the fall term of the present year of 1956." Judge Taylor says the Supreme Court's rulings in *Brown I* and *Brown II* require this outcome.

....

February 1956 When Autherine Lucy becomes the first African American to enroll at the University of Alabama, white student mobs erupt in riots. The university expels Lucy, citing her criticism of the school.

....

August 1956 The Clinton 12 begin their school year at Clinton High School.

....

November 1956 The U.S. Supreme Court rules that segregation on public buses violates the Fourteenth Amendment to the U.S. Constitution. The case is *Browder v. Gayle*. After the decision, the city of Montgomery, Alabama, stops enforcing its bus segregation laws, and organizers of the Montgomery Bus Boycott call off their boycott, which had been in effect for 381 days.

....

November 1956 Black students at Clinton High School stay home from school because of harassment and violence against them by whites.

....

December 1956 Clinton High School closes after the assault on Reverend Paul Turner when he walks the African American students back to school. A week later, the school reopens.

....

September 1957 When nine African American students attempt to enter Central High School in Little Rock, Arkansas, in compliance with a court-ordered desegregation plan, white mobs threaten their safety. The governor of Arkansas, Orval Faubus, instructs the Arkansas National Guard to turn the black students away. Weeks later, the mayor of Little Rock asks for assistance in carrying out desegregation from President Dwight D. Eisenhower. The president takes control of the National Guard in Arkansas, ordering the troops to support and not hinder integration, and also sends in the 101st Airborne Division of the U.S. Army. The Little Rock 9 finally enter the school under military protection. Soldiers remain at Central High School throughout the school year.

....

September 1958 Arkansas Governor Orval Faubus shuts down all high schools in Little Rock, invoking a law newly passed by the Arkansas General Assembly to fend off desegregation.

....

October 1958 A powerful dynamite blast destroys most of Clinton High School. The school is empty at the time of the explosion, so no one is hurt. A few days later, students take buses to an empty elementary school in Oak Ridge, Tennessee, which becomes their high school until Clinton High can be rebuilt.

....

October 1958 Ten thousand people, including many students, conduct the Youth March for Integrated Schools in Washington, DC.

....

April 1959 A second Youth March for Integrated Schools converges on Washington, DC, with 26,000 attending to urge Congress and the president to pass laws to ensure the speedy integration of schools. No new laws result from these requests.

....

June 1959 The government of Prince Edward County, Virginia, shuts down its public school system rather than submit to court-ordered integration. Schools stayed closed for five years.

....

August 1959 After a year of no public schooling, high schools reopen in Little Rock, Arkansas. Most members of the Little Rock 9 did not return to Central High.

....

February 1960 Four black students refuse to leave a segregated lunch counter after being denied service at a Woolworth store in Greensboro, North Carolina, setting off a movement of "sit-ins" at other segregated venues across the country.

....

September 1960 The newly rebuilt Clinton High School reopens.

....

November 1960 Six-year-old Ruby Bridges integrates William Frantz Public School in New Orleans, Louisiana. U.S. Marshals accompany Ruby to shield her from angry whites on her first day and every subsequent day of the school year. Many white parents withdraw their children from the school, and Ruby is placed in a first-grade class by herself, taught by Barbara Henry. Neither of them missed a day of school that year.

....

Summer 1961 Black and white "Freedom Riders" travel throughout the South on buses to protest segregation in transportation and at bus stations.

....

October 1962 James Meredith, an African American veteran of the U.S. Air Force, becomes the first black student to enroll in the University of Mississippi—also known as "Ole Miss"—in Oxford, Mississippi. Leading up to Meredith's court-ordered admittance, Governor Ross Barnett vows that no school in the state will be integrated, and encourages white people to resist. President John F. Kennedy sends federal troops to the campus. White rioters mass on school grounds and engage in violence; two men are killed. Some historians later dub the violence "the last battle of the Civil

War." Meredith, however, begins classes. He is guarded by U.S. troops throughout his college career and successfully graduates.

....

June 1963 James Alexander Hood and Vivian Juanita Malone, two African American students, are scheduled to register at the University of Alabama—the same school that expelled Autherine Lucy in 1956. The state's segregationist governor, George Wallace, surrounds himself with Alabama state troopers and stands at the door to the university, barring the two students and an official from the U.S. Department of Justice from entering. President Kennedy orders the Alabama National Guard to the school to force Wallace to step aside and allow the students to enroll.

....

August 1963 Thousands of people come to the nation's capital for the March on Washington for Jobs and Freedom. At this historic gathering of 250,000 people, Dr. Martin Luther King Jr. gives his famous "I Have a Dream" speech.

....

September 1963 In Birmingham, Alabama, the 16th Street Baptist Church is bombed, killing four African American girls: Addie Mae Collins, Denise McNair, Carole Robertson, and Cynthia Wesley. The church is a meeting place for civil rights leaders.

....

July 1964 President Lyndon Baines Johnson signs the Civil Rights Act of 1964, which, among other things, prohibits discrimination in public schools and authorizes the federal government to file lawsuits against racially segregated schools.

....

March 1965 Six hundred people set out to march from Selma to Montgomery, Alabama, to protest the denial of voting rights to black citizens. Alabama police attack the marchers with clubs, whips, and tear gas. The day becomes known as "Bloody

Sunday." President Johnson responds with a speech decrying racial prejudice and injustice.

....

August 1965 President Johnson signs into law the Voting Rights Act of 1965, guaranteeing African Americans the right to vote in elections.

....

October 1967 Nominated by President Johnson, Thurgood Marshall becomes the first African American justice of the U.S. Supreme Court. Earlier in his career, as a civil rights lawyer, Marshall was involved in many school desegregation cases—including the *McSwain* case in Clinton, Tennessee.

....

April 1968 Dr. Martin Luther King Jr. is assassinated in Memphis, Tennessee.

....

May 1968 In a case addressing the failure of many school systems to desegregate their schools, the Supreme Court says that *Brown v. Board* means that school systems are obligated to eliminate racial desegregation "root and branch" (*Green v. County School Board of New Kent County*).

....

October 1969 The U.S. Supreme Court says, fifteen years after *Brown v. Board*, that school districts must stop delaying the implementation of full school integration. The Court's opinion states: "continued operation of segregated schools under a standard of allowing 'all deliberate speed' for desegregation is no longer constitutionally permissible" (*Alexander v. Holmes County Board of Education*).

....

Today, school segregation still persists in many parts of the United States.

ACKNOWLEDGMENTS

Thank you to Anna Theresser Caswell, Mamie Allen Hubbard, Jerry Shattuck, and Gail Ann Upton (Epps) for hours of interviews, in person and over the telephone. Many thanks to Minnie Ann Jones (Dickey), Alvah Jay Lambert (McSwain), and Regina Smith (Turner) for helpful conversations as well.

Many thanks to Marilyn Hayden of the Green McAdoo Cultural Center for opening the museum's doors to us on its official "closed" day, and for research assistance.

Thank you to Ben Hoffman for invaluable feedback on the manuscript that became this book. Much gratitude also to Beth Kephart, whose comments and encouragement on early chapters were so important, and to Charlotte Nicole Davis for perceptive insights as the manuscript neared its final form. Thanks as well to Libby Boyce, whose abiding interest in the Clinton 12 sparked the idea for this book. We're also grateful to Ekua Holmes for creating the gorgeous art for our book jacket.

Finally, many thanks to our literary agent, Caryn Wiseman, and to the team at Bloomsbury Children's Books—most notably our editor, Susan Dobinick, Diane Aronson, Melissa Kavonic, Donna Mark, Danielle Ceccolini, Beth Eller, Elizabeth Mason, Erica Loberg, Phoebe Dyer, Cindy Loh, and Annette Pollert-Morgan.

QUOTATION SOURCES

19 "No school established": Constitution of Tennessee. Pauli Murray, ed., *States' Laws on Race and Color* (Athens, GA: University of Georgia Press, 1997), page 427, and *McSwain v. County Board of Education*, 104 F. Supp. 861 (E.D. Tenn. 1952).

25–26 "Section 11395": Code of Tennessee. *McSwain v. County Board of Education*, 104 F. Supp. 861 (E.D. Tenn. 1952).

29 "We conclude that": Written opinion of U.S. Supreme Court in *Brown v. Board of Education*, 347 U.S. 483 (1954).

30 "It is the opinion": Written opinion of Judge Taylor in *McSwain v. County Board of Education*, 138 F. Supp. 570 (E.D. Tenn. 1956).

43 "I come to the garden": "In The Garden," by C. Austin Miles, 1912.

67 "Help us": Prayer led by Reverend O.W. Willis, Mt. Sinai Baptist Church, Sunday night, August 26, 1956, quoted in George McMillan, "The Ordeal of Bobby Cain," *Collier's*, November 23, 1956.

71 "We won't go": AP Image 560827031.

72 "We the pupils": AP Image 560827031.

81 "It's just that": George Barrett, "Study in Desegregation: The Clinton Story," *New York Times Magazine*, September 16, 1956.

89 "You and your people": Anna Holden, Bonita Valien, and Preston Valien, "Clinton, Tennessee: A Tentative Description and Analysis of the School Desegregation Crisis." NY: Anti-Defamation League of B'nai B'rith, p. 21.

122 **"There is no danger"**: P-TA notice quoted in "Clinton P-TA Urges Pupils To Return," *Clinton Courier-News*, September 6, 1956.

128 **"It's the Sabbath"**: "Negroes of Clinton Mum," *Washington Post*, September 4, 1956.

128 **"Those instigating"**: "Sentence Mob Chief To A Year: Judge gets tough with agitators," *Baltimore Afro-American*, September 8, 1956.

133 **"First, let me say"**: Statement of Mayor W.E. Lewallen in "Clinton Mayor Tells Tribune Reporter Supreme Court Decision 'Bitter Dose,'" *Philadelphia Tribune*, September 22, 1956.

154 **"Jo Ann asked"**: "Clinton Pupils say President 'should use his authority,'" *Baltimore Afro-American*, October 6, 1956.

156 **"President Eisenhower"**: "Clinton Pupils say President 'should use his authority,'" *Baltimore Afro-American*, October 6, 1956.

183 **"He speaks"**: "In The Garden," by C. Austin Miles, 1912.

197 **"We don't want to"**: Rachel L. Martin. "Out of the Silence: Remembering the Desegregation of Clinton, Tennessee, High School: A dissertation submitted to the faculty of the University of North Carolina at Chapel Hill," 2012, p. 285.

210 **"We want"**: *Oak Ridger*, November 29, 1956, and "Negroes at Clinton Ask Safety Pledge," *New York Times*, December 1, 1956.

218 **"Let's get"**: "U.S. To Prosecute Clinton Balkers of School Decree," *New York Times*, December 5, 1956.

218 **"We are going to"**: Principal Brittain's statement reprinted in Margaret Anderson, *The Children of the South* (New York: Farrar, Strauss and Giroux, 1966), p. 19.

231 **"I thought":** Margaret Anderson, *The Children of the South*, p. 19.

235 **"barring any":** "Clinton Outlines Curbs for Pupils," *New York Times*, December 8, 1956.

243 **"They put signs":** *See It Now: Clinton and the Law*, CBS broadcast of January 6, 1957, https://youtu.be/WgGXc8vSfIU, at 11:39 minutes.

243 **"We're not":** *See It Now: Clinton and the Law*, CBS broadcast of January 6, 1957, https://youtu.be/WgGXc8vSfIU, at 48:27 minutes.

245 **"We are not especially":** *See It Now: Clinton and the Law*, CBS broadcast of January 6, 1957, https://youtu.be/WgGXc8vSfIU, at 40:00 minutes.

246 **"I accompanied the Negro students":** Margaret Anderson, *The Children of the South*, p. 20.

254–55 **"Here's why Jo Ann":** *Chicago Defender*, December 10, 1956. Courtesy of the *Chicago Defender*.

257 **"It is not my intention":** *See It Now: Clinton and the Law*, CBS broadcast of January 6, 1957, https://youtu.be/WgGXc8vSfIU, at 41:05 minutes.

258 **"I can frankly":** Margaret Anderson, *The Children of the South*, p. 21.

260 **"We are one":** *Courier News Special Commemorative Edition* [Clinton, TN], August 26, 2006.

262 **"Of all the integration hotspots":** "Cool Spot in Tennessee," *Time*, September 16, 1957.

262 **"Mob violence":** Margaret Anderson, "The South Learns Its Hardest Lessons," *New York Times Magazine*, September 11, 1960.

265 **"I want to tell you":** "A Tennessee Town Marks Desegregation," *Washington Post*, October 15, 2006.

266 "That was one": Green McAdoo Cultural Center, http://www.greenmcadoo.org/about-the-center.

267 "It was lonely": Interview with Debbie Levy and Jo Ann Allen Boyce, May 2, 2017.

267 "I was jumpy": "'It was scary to go to school everyday,'" *The Call* (published by Holston Conference of the United Methodist Church), February 11, 2005.

268 "I was wondering": "Progress measured in steps," *Knoxville News Sentinel*, August 27, 2006.

268 "I lived": Telephone interview with Debbie Levy, January 30, 2017.

268 "The Clinton desegregation": Green McAdoo Cultural Center, http://www.greenmcadoo.org/about-the-center.

269 "I really": Green McAdoo Cultural Center, http://www.greenmcadoo.org/about-the-center.

269 "In Clinton it was": June N. Adamson, "Few Black Voices Heard: The Black Community and the Desegregation Crisis in Clinton, Tennessee, 1956," *Tennessee Historical Quarterly*, Spring 1994, p. 37.

278 "I have almost reached": "Letter from a Birmingham Jail," The Martin Luther King, Jr. Research and Education Institute, Stanford University, https://kinginstitute.stanford.edu/king-papers/documents/letter-birmingham-jail.

SELECTED BIBLIOGRAPHY

ARTICLES, BOOKS, PAPERS, AND WEBSITES

June N. Adamson. "Few Black Voices Heard: The Black Community and the Desegregation Crisis in Clinton, Tennessee, 1956." *Tennessee Historical Quarterly*, Spring 1994.

Margaret Anderson. "Clinton, Tenn.: Children in a Crucible." *New York Times Magazine*, November 2, 1958.

_____. *The Children of the South*. NY: Farrar, Straus and Giroux, 1968.

_____. "The South Learns Its Hardest Lessons." *New York Times Magazine*, September 11, 1960.

George Barrett, "Study in Desegregation: The Clinton Story." *New York Times Magazine*, September 16, 1956.

David J. Brittain. "A Case Study of the Problems of Racial Integration in the Clinton, Tennessee High School: Submitted in partial fulfillment of the requirements for the degree of Doctor of Education in the School of Education of New York University" (1959).

_____. "What School People Have Learned about Integration." *Educational Leadership*, May 1958.

Whitney Elizabeth Cate. "Forgotten Heroes: Lessons from School Integration in a Small Southern Community: A thesis presented to the faculty of the Department of History, East Tennessee State University" (2012). *Electronic Theses and Dissertations*. Paper 1512. http://dc.etsu.edu/etd/1512.

Doug Davis. *Gifts Given: Family, Community, and Integration's Move from the Courtroom to the Schoolyard*. iUniverse: 2012.

Heather Flood. "Chaos in Clinton: A thesis presented to the faculty of the Department of History, East Tennessee State University" (2007). *Electronic Theses and Dissertations*. Paper 2148. http://dc.etsu.edu/2148.

Green McAdoo Cultural Organization. National Register of Historic Places Registration Form for Green McAdoo School. September 22, 2005.

Green McAdoo Cultural Center website. http://www.greenmcadoo.org/story.

David Halberstam, "The Town That Became 'Everybody's Test Tube.'" *The Reporter*, January 10, 1957.

Anna Holden, Bonita Valien, and Preston Valien, "Clinton, Tennessee: A Tentative Description and Analysis of the School Desegregation Crisis." NY: Anti-Defamation League of B'nai B'rith. n.d.

Rachel L. Martin. "Out of the Silence: Remembering the Desegregation of Clinton, Tennessee, High School: A dissertation submitted to the faculty of the University of North Carolina at Chapel Hill," 2012.

_____. "To Go to the Richy Kreme." https://rachelmartin.wordpress.com/2015/10/07/to-go-to-the-richy-kreme/.

_____. "That Opportunity Was Lost, an Interview with Jo Ann Allen Boyce." https://rachelmartin.wordpress.com/20115/09/01/that-opportunity-was-lost-an-interview-with-jo-ann-allen-boyce.

_____. "The Brave and Tragic Trail of Reverend Turner." http://narratively/the-brave-and-tragic-trail-of-reverend-turner/.

George McMillan. "The Ordeal of Bobby Cain." *Collier's Weekly*, November 23, 1956.

Neil R. McMillen. "Organized Resistance to School Desegregation in Tennessee." *Tennessee Historical Quarterly*, Fall 1971.

Lana Carmen Seivers. "Words of Discrimination, Voices of Determination: Reflections on the Desegregation of Clinton High School: A Dissertation Presented for the Doctor of Education Degree, the University of Tennessee, Knoxville," May 2002.

D. Ray Smith. "McSwain sisters tell the story that predated the Clinton 12." *Oak Ridger*, September 6, 2006.

Carroll Van West. "Clinton Desegregation Crisis." *Tennessee Encyclopedia of History and Culture*. Online at http://www .tennesseeencyclopedia.net/imagegallery.php?EntryID=C111.

In addition to the sources specified above, numerous articles from the following newspapers and magazines that covered events in Clinton from 1956 through 1958 were consulted: *Atlanta Daily World, Baltimore Afro-American, Chicago Defender, Clinton Courier-News, Knoxville Journal, Los Angeles Sentinel, Los Angeles Times, New York Times, Norfolk New Journal and Guide, Oak Ridger, Philadelphia Tribune, Pittsburgh Courier, Time,* and *Washington Post.* Also helpful was a series of articles entitled "The Green McAdoo Series," published in Clinton's *Courier News* in 2006 in the months leading up to the fiftieth anniversary of the desegregation of Clinton High School and to the opening of the Green McAdoo Cultural Center.

VIDEO AND FILM

"Cameron Boyce Honors The Clinton 12," Disney XD. https:// youtu.be/fgSKSeuTLAk

The Clinton 12: A Documentary Film. Directed by Keith McDaniel. Green McAdoo Cultural Organization and Secret City Films & HP Video, Inc., 2007.

"The Clinton 12." Video by National Education Association. https://youtu.be/tvOJRQPKmE4

"Clinton and the Law." CBS broadcast of *See It Now*, January 6, 1957. https://youtu.be/WgGXc8vSfIU

JUDICIAL OPINIONS
Brown v. Board of Education of Topeka, 347 U.S. 483 (1954).

Brown v. Board of Education of Topeka (*Brown* II), 349 U.S. 294 (1955).

McSwain v. County Board of Education of Anderson County, 104 F. Supp. 861 (E.D. Tenn. 1952).

McSwain v. County Board of Education of Anderson County, 138 F. Supp. 570 (E.D. Tenn. 1956).

INTERVIEWS
Anna Theresser Caswell. With Jo Ann Allen Boyce and Debbie Levy, May 2, 2017, Claxton, Tennessee.

Mamie Allen Hubbard. Telephone interview with Debbie Levy, February 21, 2017.

Jerry Shattuck. Telephone interview with Debbie Levy, February 21, 2017.

Gail Ann Upton (Epps). Telephone interview with Debbie Levy, January 30, 2017.

_____. With Jo Ann Allen Boyce and Debbie Levy, May 1, 2017, Sweetwater, Tennessee.

FURTHER READING

Daisy Bates, *The Long Shadow of Little Rock: A Memoir*. University of Arkansas Press, 2007.

Melba Patillo Beals. *Warriors Don't Cry*. New York: Simon Pulse, 2007.

Dennis Brindell Fradin and Judith Bloom Fradin. *The Power of One: Daisy Bates and the Little Rock Nine*. New York: Clarion Books, 2004.

Phillip Hoose. *Claudette Colvin: Twice Toward Justice*. New York: Farrar Straus Giroux Books for Young Readers, 2014.

Cynthia Levinson. *We've Got a Job: The 1963 Birmingham Children's March*. Atlanta: Peachtree Publishers, 2012.

Library of Congress. "Civil Rights History Project." https://www.loc.gov/collections/civil-rights-history-project/.

Library of Congress. "Brown v. Board at Fifty: 'With an Even Hand.'" http://www.loc.gov/exhibits/brown/brown-aftermath.html.

Toni Morrison. *Remember: The Journey to School Desegregation*. New York: HMH Books for Young Readers, 2004.

Patricia Hruby Powell and Shadra Strickland (illustrator). *Loving vs. Virginia: A Documentary Novel of the Landmark Civil Rights Case*. San Francisco: Chronicle Books, 2017.

PBS, "Supreme Court History: Expanding Civil Rights." http://www.thirteen.org/wnet/supremecourt/rights/index.html.

PBS, "The Rise and Fall of Jim Crow." http://www.thirteen.org/wnet/jimcrow/.

PHOTOGRAPH CREDITS

Photos by Robert W. Kelley/The LIFE Picture Collection/Getty Images: 279; 281, bottom; 282; 284, top and bottom; 285, top. Photos by Howard Sochurek/The LIFE Picture Collection/Getty Images: 280, top; 281, top; 286. Photos from Associated Press: 280, bottom; 283; 285, bottom. Photos by Don Cravens/The LIFE Images Collection/Getty Images: 287; 288, top; 289. Courtesy of the authors: 288, bottom; 290, top and bottom.